I0558265

Axolotl

A Personal Journey of Helpful Learnings

(Everything You Need to Know Before You Keep Axolotls)

Douglas Johnson

Published By **Elena Holly**

Douglas Johnson

All Rights Reserved

Axolotl: A Personal Journey of Helpful Learnings (Everything You Need to Know Before You Keep Axolotls)

ISBN   978-1-990373-79-4

No part of this guidebook shall be reproduced in any form without permission in writing from the publisher except in the case of brief quotations embodied in critical articles or reviews.

Legal & Disclaimer

The information contained in this book is not designed to replace or take the place of any form of medicine or professional medical advice. The information in this book has been provided for educational & entertainment purposes only.

The information contained in this book has been compiled from sources deemed reliable, and it is accurate to the best of the Author's knowledge; however, the Author cannot guarantee its accuracy and validity and cannot be held liable for any errors or omissions. Changes are periodically made to this book. You must consult your doctor or get professional medical advice before using any of the suggested remedies, techniques, or information in this book.

Upon using the information contained in this book, you agree to hold harmless the Author from and against any damages, costs, and expenses, including any legal fees potentially resulting from the application of any of the information provided by this guide. This disclaimer applies to any damages or injury caused by the use and application, whether directly or indirectly, of any advice or information presented, whether for breach of contract, tort, negligence, personal injury, criminal intent, or under any other cause of action.

You agree to accept all risks of using the information presented inside this book. You need to consult a professional medical practitioner in order to ensure you are both able and healthy enough to participate in this program.

Table Of Contents

Chapter 1: Your Guide To Keeping Axolotl As A Pet

Everything you've ever wanted learn about this adorable amphibian

This adorable creature originates from Mexico and derives it's name after the Aztec god of lightning and fire, Xolotl.

According to the legend, Xolotl changed into an axolotl in order to avoid being killed.

The trick was unsuccessful and he eventually died The axolotl remains an iconic animal that has been captivating people throughout the ages.

The amphibian is defying biological rules like metamorphosis, and may even regenerate body parts that have been lost and organs, which makes it a crucial area of study in labs all over the world.

What is the meaning of an Axolotl?

The axolotl salamander is one species.

Salamanders are an amphibian. They are also known as the frogs, newts, and toads.

The Amphibians depend on water for reproduction (although there are plenty species that have developed an ingenious method of getting over this).

The eggs will be laid in the water and then the larvae hatch, and then gradually change into an adult capable of surviving on land.

Axolotls are, on the other on the other hand, are never mature.

The term 'neotenous' refers to them as this means they are not transformed into lung-breathing land dwellers in the same way that amphibians generally do.

Instead the animals retain characteristics from their youth including tails, gills as well as a preference to live in water.

How do axolotls appear?

Axolotls are amazing... as well as strange due to their hairless heads with button eyes and their gummy smiles.

Adult axolotls range from 30cm long from the the tip of their noses to the tail end, with the biggest species reaching 45 centimeters.

They could weigh as much as 300 grams.

In addition to their hefty bodies and limbs with a comically short length They also sport unusual headwear made of gills with feathers that define their adorable faces.

Gills like these - additionally present in various species of young amphibians permit them to take oxygen from the water to allow them to breathe.

In addition to their gills the axolotls' lungs are tiny They are often found at the top of the water in small breaths.

How do they make their homes?

The only Mexico City's Lake Xochimilco is home to the Axolotl.

This region is high-altitude that rarely exceeds 20degC in water temperatures.

The people also lived within Lake Chalco, but that lake was dewatered in the 1970s in order to avoid flooding.

The population is declining due to pollution as well as the impact from Mexico City on their habitat.

Furthermore, the freshwater fish that are introduced devour axolotl eggs, and are more apt to predators of insects.

Are axolotls at risk of extinction?

Axolotls are classified as extremely endangered on the IUCN Red List of threatened species.

Axolotls as per an article released in BioScience has suffered massive decline over the past few years.

Dr. Luis Zambrano Gonzalez counted 6,000 Axolotls per square mile in 1998.

In 2008, there were less than 100 amphibians per square km.

Based on more recent statistics it is less than 36 people per square kilometer.

In addition, captive populations flourish in labs across the globe The adorable amphibians can be wonderful pets.

A plethora of players became familiar with these creatures over the last few years, following their introduction as characters to play in Fortnite in the year 2020.

Axolotls were discovered the next year. were found in the lush caves biome of Minecraft.

Can we bring back axolotls?

"The primary point to emphasize is the fact that wild axolotls are not able to be saved without restoration of their habitats.

So, prior to reintroducing the need to rebuild the wetland to ensure the safety of axolotls their natural habitat.

Every attempt to introduce axolotls are not working because of this," Zambrano Gonzalez explains.

"We have restored the ecosystem because it's integrally linked to pre-Columbian cultures.

This and many other reasons such as the decline in genetic diversity as well as the introduction of axolotl disease - it's not advisable to begin an invasive reintroduction programme that is captive-bred."

Based on Zambrano Gonzalez and other authors Zambrano Gonzalez and others, the first essential phase in the development of axolotl refuges is to improve water quality.

The change will benefit native species like the axolotl, while benefiting the crops. This makes it a viable alternative for farmers.

Are axolotls interesting for researchers?

Since the year 1863, the year they first came into Paris from Mexico The strange creatures have captivated researchers.

If animals suffer injuries Researchers have found that they are able to regenerate entire limbs eyes the heart, parts of the brain, as well as the spinal cord, returning these body parts back to functioning.

They even will accept legs transplanted by other people.

When an axolotl is exposed to thyroid hormones it's possible to trigger metamorphosis.

But, as per studies published in Scientific Reports in 2018, it could affect the capacity of animals to regenerate and could also alter its microbiome.

Nature released a research study where the genome of the axolotl was sequenced up to 32 billion base pairs, which is 10 times larger than Human genome.

It was the most massive genome of all animals at the time. It was later overtaken by the lungfish with a genome that is 43 billion base pair.

The genome of the organism revealed sequences which appear to play an important role in the process of regeneration of the limb.

What is the food that axolotls take?

Axolotls can eat almost all things that fit into their mouths!

They consume bugs, worms, crustaceans, as well as small wild fish.

Also, they are cannibalistic creatures that eat each other when food sources are limited.

Axolotls are kept as pets, or as laboratory animals receive worms, shrimp or fragments of fish.

Because of their teeth that aren't fully developed The animals eat through sucking small objects in their mouths.

Axolotls' popularity pets has led to the development of various color-related morphs including this golden example.

What color can you find in an Axolotl?

Axolotls from the wild kind' typically have grayish-green in color.

It is in stark contrast with the animals that are that are sold for pets. They tend to be pinkish, with black eyes and red gills.

In light of the growing popularity of pets like axolotls and pets, selective breeding has led to the creation of many color variations, such as albino, golden and speckled.

How long will it last for the axolotls?

Axolotls can live up to 10-15 years, with the possibility of a little longer if they are properly looked after in captive.

What's the look of a child axolotl?

Axolotl embryos, just like Frog embryos, are enclosed in a jelly-like material.

The baby axolotl is visible through the goo. The axolotl develops in 14-30 days subject to the temperature of the water.

The moment the baby axolotls hatch they are born with feathery gills as well as the long tail is like adults but with no legs.

Around a month the age of about a month, they'll have grown legs and look like the size of a tiny adult.

An oddity that is well-known

Axolotls are a favorite of the imagination of all who see them, more so after their arrival to Mexico to Paris in 1864.

Europeans started breeding salamanders across Europe, which marked the beginning of a flourishing trade in the animal's fur and they breed quickly when kept in captive.

They're mostly dark brown to grayish on the open field.

Axolotls that have lighter hues and pink gills and white bodies usually breed to be pets.

Yet, the species is not allowed to be trade across borders internationally across the vast majority of nations partly due to fears of poaching in wild.

Axolotls are banned in certain states of the United States for the same justification.

Some states of the United States prohibit the ownership of axolotls in order to reduce the possibility of their escape from in captivity and interbreeding salamanders.

Axolotls can also be a very popular topic of research for biologists because of their capacity to regenerate missing and damaged parts of limbs heart or spinal cords even a portion of their brains, without permanently causing damage.

As scarring can hinder the growth of tissues Understanding why and how the axolotls don't scar can aid humans in regaining their capacity to replenish tissues.

In April, for instance, a 2021 research study revealed how Axolotl's molecules interact to stimulate the process of regeneration.

Despite the fact that they are kept in a wide range of captivity, Axolotls living in the wild are in serious danger.

Amphibians used to live in the high-altitude lakes that surround Mexico City, but habitat decline has slowed their spread to a handful of in the canals located in the inland.

Reproduction

Axolotls are small, solitary animals who reach sexual maturity around the age of one year and then spawn in February.

Males draw females by the use of pheromones. dance an obscene relationship "hula" dance, shaking his tail as well as his lower body.

She responds by nudging from her mouth.

Males then deposit Spermatophores, also known as sperm packets on the floor of the lake and the female collects with her cloaca or body cavity, and fertilizes her eggs.

Females may lay up to 1000 eggs (though an average of 300) This protects their eggs from predators.

The eggs hatch within two weeks and, if they are not under the supervision of a parent the larvae have gone floating around by themselves.

There's a theory as the reason why adult axolotls do not appear different.

As their natural lakes don't get dry, like other water bodies do, axolotls didn't require the exchange of the characteristics of water, like the tail of a tadpole for features of terrestrial nature, such as legs.

Conservation

Based on a report from 2019 of the International Union for the Conservation of Species There are just 50 to 1,000 wild axolotls in the wild, and their numbers are decreasing.

Residential and tourism development together with industrial and agricultural pollution, has led to an alarming decline in number of species.

Tilapia's introduction as well as other fish that consume baby salamanders and fight to eat with adults have had the same impact.

Chapter 2: Axolotl Breeds

Axolotl Colors: Axolotl Morphologies

Based on our study we have identified the following axolotl varieties:

* Golden albino* White albino * leucistic albino Pibald albino * Copper * black melanoid albino, Lavender * Firefly * Chimera Mosaic

The axolotl was named in honor of the legend of an Aztec god of lightning and fire, is a unique aquatic salamander that is only found naturally within Mexico City's lakes system.

The axolotl may be related to the salamander tiger it's also one of the most distinctive amphibians found on earth.

It matures and reaches adulthood but will never undergo metamorphosis.

It is also known as neoteny. It is a reference to the fact that adults retain several characteristics that are characteristic of larvae like Gill stalks, and the capability to stay within the water.

Furthermore, it has the ability to regenerate the limbs as well as other organs quickly and has stimulated an intense studies.

This animal can be identified through its dark or light brown skin and gold flecks all over the body wild.

The axolotl, a species that is endangered in its natural habitat human beings can cultivate it in captivity for reasons of scientific and commercial research.

Artificial selection (i.e. an evolution driven by human beings) has led to a variety of variations of axolotl with distinctive dimensions, shapes, as well as colors compared to wild types.

Now you can locate an aqua axolotl which is both physically and visually acceptable to your tastes.

This book will explore some of the interesting Axolotl colours, the rare and common variants.

The more rare axolotl shades are somewhat harder to find and are generally more costly in comparison to the standard ones.

Axolotls cost around $40-$50 and upwards in cost after that.

Certain colours of axolotls can be uncommon and could be priced as high as $1,000.

10. Axolotl albino blanco

The white albino's hue is caused by a low level of melanin.

The albino white axolotl is among the color morphs that are more commonly used.

The albino form is identified by the pure white appearance of its body and red gill filaments and white or pink eyes. The reason for this is the axolotl producing a lot lower levels of melanin. It is a pigment that is not just responsible for skin's color, but also protects the skin from harmful UV rays.

Furthermore, it is deficient in important pigments within the eye.

In the end, this type of morph is thought as extremely sensitive to light.

The animal would likely be a struggle in wild conditions, but humans have benefited from the skin color of albino and added more albinos that are kept in captivity.

For being an albino the offspring of albinos must carry two copies of recessive albino gene. One copy is not a factor in the skin's color.

The albino's appearance variations as they grow older.

Although the body stays completely white, the color of the gill stalks is likely to get more intense.

9. Axolotl that has a coloration leucistic

The speckled leucistic morph is similar to the skin color of the leucistic axolotl.

Although the leucistic axolotl might appear to be an albino on first sight but it's actually more translucent skin that is transparent, sporting red filaments in the gills as well as dark brown eyes or black.

The main biological difference is that the albino variation can be created through reducing just melanin pigment, while the leucistic variation is made through the reduction of all pigments within the skin.

The speckled leucistic type is the same skin color as the transparent leucistic form but with dark brown, green or black speckles over the body, back, or the tail.

The larvae start by displaying a typical leucistic form however, they develop speckles when the pigment cells develop.

The speckled and leucistic forms are fairly commonplace within the pet trade of axolotl.

8: Axolotl Piebald

The piebald color is considered to be one of the rarest axolotl hues.

The cause is a partial leucism, in which black or dark green patches or spots cover a large area of the transparent skin that is white.

The vast majority of patches cover the face as well as the back. Only some that cover the legs and sides.

It's distinguished from the leucistic speckled morph because of the number of spots that appear on the body.

The spots on the skin can become darker in time, and eventually cover the entire skin with the white and black markings.

The gene that is which is the cause of this pattern may be acquired, but it's extremely rare.

7. Axolotl Golden albino

Golden albino is an extremely popular color used for the artificial Axolotls.

Golden albino is one of the most commonly used synthetic axolotl shades.

Its bright gold skin (along with pink, white or yellow eyes, as well as reflective patches on the body) and gradually changes in the color of its body from white and finally orange-gold throughout its life.

The golden albino larvae are born it is nearly impossible to distinguish them from albino larvae. However, at the time they reach the point of death the golden hue becomes extremely shiny.

This color shift result from the reduction of most pigments, with the exception of one that is that is responsible for gold and yellow.

6. Copper Axolotl

This morph, which is not very common, features a body that is light gray-green with copper-colored flecks that are evenly dispersed on the skin's face.

It also has grey eyes, and gray-red gills.

The unique pattern is due to a decrease in melanin as well as other levels of pigment on the skin.

Copper morphs are typically seen throughout the United States and Australia; They are not common elsewhere.

They are able to create fascinating combinations when cross-bred with morphs from other types.

5. Axolotl melanoid noir

Black melanoid axolotl was identified by chance in the year 1961.

The black melanoid was first discovered in the year 1961, and since then has grown into one of the more popular color morphs found on the world.

Because of the distinctive coloring of its skin it shows a range from dark green to black transformations, with deep purple gills as well as the appearance of a light grey or purple belly.

Certain species resemble wild-type Axolotls with the exception of the golden Iris.

The black color morph is almost exactly the same as the albino color.

4. Axolotl in lavender

This color variation is defined by a light silvery purple hue, aswell being gray-red gills, and eyes with black that change to green or gray.

In light of the existence of spots all over the body, it's sometimes referred to as the Dalmatian axolotl.

Even though these color morphs can be more difficult to come across and are more costly than normal color morphs they are distinctive.

3. Axolotl and 3: Axolotl with Firefly

It is without any doubt, the most debated morph.

The morph of the firefly is wild-type dark-colored axolotl which has an albino-colored tail, which shines in darkness when it is exposed to black light. The reason for this is being surrounded by a fluorescent green protein.

Chapter 3: How To Create An Axolotl Tank: A Step-By-Step Guide To Setup And Care

Axolotls (Ambystoma mexicanum) are not the usual inhabitants of aquariums.

Though they're often described as walking fish, they're in reality amphibians.

In particular the neotenic salamanders stay permanently stuck in their full-on aqua larval stage, and do not ever lose their gills.

Axolotls (Ambystoma mexicanum) originated in Central Mexico, more precisely within the lake areas which surround the area of Mexico City.

Their name derives from the Nahuatl native word meaning the salamanders that are unique.

In reality, they are threatened within the natural world.

The habitat of the animals has diminished to less than a quarter of their former size, in the same way that Mexico City has grown, and the pollution has become a major issue.

They are thriving in captivity, and through proper conservation they may be released back into the wild.

Do you think that was enough to spark your curiosity?

We are able to think!

Axolotl maintenance is a little different from that of other fish in aquariums.

The guide we've put together will cover everything you should learn about how to set up and maintain the Axolotl tank.

How to Build an Axolotl Tank - Equipment Required:

Everything you'll require to set up your ideal Axolotl tank is provided in the following:

How Much Tank Space Does an Axolotl Require?

The selection of the right tank is essential when starting with any aquarium animal It's the case with Axolotls.

There is unfortunately an abundance of information that is outdated regarding this species on the internet and includes information regarding the size of tanks.

Contrary to what many believe the size of a 10 gallon aquarium is not enough for an Axolotl over the long term.

Although a single specimen might be a viable alternative if you plan to build a bigger set later, given the fact that an adult's size of 10 inches isn't common, it's better choosing a more substantial setup right away.

A 20-gallon aquarium is enough to house a single Axolotl.

Remember that a tank with a longer length will be more preferable than tall ones, because they are bottom dwellers and have little requirement for vertical space.

If you want to maintain more than an Axolotl make sure you give plenty of space

10 additional gallons of water for every additional salamander is an excellent guideline.

Filtration Systems for Axolotl Tanks

Every aquarium needs an aquarium filter.

In selecting the right one to use in your Axolotl installation, bear in mind that they do not like overflowing water.

One that can be easily blocked using a piece of sponge over the outlet is an ideal option.

Axolotl people who keep their eyes on sponge filters as they efficiently filter out an excessive flow.

In order to operate this kind of filter will require an air compressor; make certain to buy a top-quality strong one that will ensure the proper filtering.

If your tank is situated in an area where people live make sure you check the level of noise prior to installation since some air pumps are extremely loud.

Do Axolotls Require Heat?

Due to the fact that Axolotls are coldwater animals which is extremely tolerant of extreme temperatures, they does not require an extremely large heater.

It is always recommended to make use of a heater in order to prevent fluctuations in temperature between night and day particularly if your aquarium is situated within a space that has frequently open windows or doors, and is susceptible to fluctuating temperatures.

How to Maintain a Cool Axolotl Tank?

The most frequently-asked question is how do you ensure that the axolotl tank at a cool temperature.

Since they are stressed when temperatures are excessively, particularly when you live in regions that experience extremely hot summers you'll need to prepare for extreme heat.

Airstones are a great method to keep your axolotl tank at a cool temperature.

In the process of forcing air into water, heat exchange can be enhanced by increasing the effective surface area in comparison to air.

In addition, airstones help to maintain the proper concentration of oxygen dissolved in the tank.

The water loses oxygen when it gets warmer.

The more airflow is better for your axolotl!

In addition, installing a blower that blows air directly over the tank's surface helps keep the axolotl in a cooler environment.

Make sure you choose to use the LED or fluorescent lighting fixtures instead of incandescent bulbs that generate lots of energy!

Kit to Test the Water in an Axolotl Tank

This is something we can't stress enough: If you plan to keep fish in your aquarium, you'll need an instrument for testing water.

It's not an exception!

A fluid (rather as strips) test kit which includes test results for ammonia/ammonium (NH3/NH4) and the nitrite (NO2) as well as the nitrate (NO3) as well as pH. allows you to check the condition of your water and make sure it's compatible with your Axolotl (s).

I highly recommend the API Freshwater Master Test Kit that is shown below.

It's (without any doubt) the most reliable test kit you can get.

Lighting for Axolotl Tanks

Make sure you choose the right lighting to the Axolotl tank.

Although many aquarists are used to using intense light for plant growth, this isn't the case for this species.

Axolotls dislike bright light and they are easily stressed by strong lamps.

Instead, you should find ways to look at your Axies, without luring the Axies into hiding for hours.

Furthermore, intense lighting especially incandescent lighting fixtures, can generate a great deal of energy.

Since axolotls like colder water, they are best served by lighting sources such as LED or fluorescent lamps that produce very little radiation infrared.

Configuring Your Axolotl Tank

If you've just decided to keep Axolotls It can be tempting to hurry to an aquarium shop to purchase one.

Unfortunately, we're compelled to ask that you exercise more patience.

Preparing and setting up everything before you receive your 'Axie(s) essential in ensuring your child's well-being and happiness.

A pet that is who is brought into a tank that has not been cycled could be a disaster!

How to Begin: Axolotl Aquarium Cycling

If all is well You can begin the process of setting up for your Axolotl tank.

Locate a room within your house that stays cool during the entire year. This will help you keep from stress and heat Axies throughout the Summer time.

The aquarium should be filled to the fullest and then turn on the required equipment, like the heater or filter.

Furthermore, you may place all your decoration (discussed in the next section) to their appropriate locations.

After that you're ready to start this cycle!

A cycle in your aquarium can allow beneficial bacteria to build up on the substrate as well as in the filter.

The bacteria in this system are the sole element that keeps your tank secure for the any future Axolotls Therefore, it is worth to spend some time on this procedure.

In order to cycle your aquarium, it is first necessary to add ammonia.

We like using unscented ammonia from the household because it's simple to use and produces little mess.

After that, adding more ammonia as required It's an issue of waiting for conducting tests..

Water Values of Axolotl

Like other inhabitants of aquariums, Axolotls thrive in a particular range of temperature and parameters.

This is important since, contrary the norms we're used to from tropical fish Axies are coldwater fish that cannot thrive in warm waters.

Temperature of Axolotl's Water

In order to maintain the health of Axolotls Aquarium temperatures should be in the range of 64 degrees Fahrenheit.

The lower temperatures are not a problem since the salamander's metabolism is likely to reduce.

The Axie can become slow with colder temperatures, but this is not an issue.

The danger of heat is much greater as well, so it is recommended to stay away from temperatures of more than 75 degrees.

In Axolotls the excessive heat creates extreme stress that could lead to illness or even death.

Axolotls are dependent on ammonia, Nitrite, as well as the nitrate.

Three of them are tied to the cycle of your body, like we have discussed before.

As you probably know Ammonia levels and nitrite levels are always zero since both can be deadly.

Nitrate is acceptable in low levels, but shouldn't be more than 15.

If you notice this, do an water change to eliminate the left-over inorganic nitrates.

What pH Preference Do Axolotls Have?

The pH test you take can be used to assess the alkalinity or acidity of the water you drink.

Axolotls are tolerant of a broad variety of pH levels that range from 6.5 and 8. 7.0 to 7.5 is the ideal range.

Water Hardness of Axolotl

Axolotls are fond of water with a relatively hard texture that is minimum 100ppm, and not greater than 200ppm.

Thankfully, the vast majority of water that is tapped in the developed world is alkaline and hard, and consequently requires no other adjustment aside from the elimination of chlorine.

Make sure to use a water tap dechlorinator in order to neutralize chlorine and chloramine prior to performing the water change.

Municipal water providers utilize these chemicals to ensure drinking water safe for consumption, they can be extremely harmful to marine life, such as Axolotls!

Choosing an Axolotl Substrate

Given that Axolotls tend to live in bottoms, it's sensible to pay careful focus on the type of substrate.

A majority of Axie supporters agree that sand is an ideal environment for amphibians.

Some also maintain Axolotls within enclosures that are bare-bottomed for convenience of cleaning, however there's some controversy about whether or not the absence of an anchor can cause an excessive amount of stress.

If you choose to have the bottom that is unfinished, you could consider the use of tiles or slate to add grip to the Axolotl (s).

Stones, gravel, and even marbles are not allowed to Axolotls.

The salamanders consider almost everything as food, and they are known to be awkward when it comes to eating.

There's a good chance that they'll get an ounce of substratum.

The issue isn't a big one for those who keep them in sand because the Axolotl is able to easily expel the sand that it eats.

But any material with larger grains could cause issues.

Ingestion of gravel could cause compaction or even death. Therefore, beware of it!

It's not worth the risk even though it is more effective at hiding waste than sand.

Decorations for Axolotl Tanks

Axolotls are fond of hiding areas and they will love aquarium decoration.

Although not every conventional aquarium décor will fit however, there's numerous options to bring some color into the look of your Axie aquarium.

Axolotl Tank Plants

We love living plants as they are not just beautiful however, they can also help to improve your water's stability worth.

Select a robust plant to fill Your Axolotl tank.

Axies aren't the kindest creatures and have been reported to rip up or crush delicate plants.

In addition, it is difficult to locate species that are able to tolerate the cold temperatures needed for Axolotls.

Marimo Moss balls are a well-known choice of Axolotl aquariums.

They, along with Axolotls are drawn to cooler water temperatures, need very little lighting, they are incredibly easily to care for (just be sure that the moss balls are big enough to not fit inside the mouth of an curious Axolotl).

Make sure to do regular water changes and also tank maintenance as maintenance of the tank, because Marimo moss balls can be extremely sensitive to the high levels of pollutants and could be smothered by algae.

Other plants that could be effective include:

Plants floating on the water can help in creating dim lighting that makes the smoky Axolotl experience more comfortable.

Additionally, they employ fertilizers such as ammonia, nitrogen, and nitrate, to help in improving the quality of water used by tanks.

A final point is that An Axolotl won't be able to harm them by cutting their roots accidentally, as they are able to do with many sub-soil-rooted plants!

In an Axolotl Tank, Driftwood

A couple of carefully set pieces of driftwood will provide a natural appearance within your tank. These pieces can also be used as hideouts.

The most suitable type of driftwood to use is big, soft driftwood without sharp edges. Avoid any material that salamander(s) may get stuck inside.

Both Cholla as well as Mopani wood look beautiful as well as useful.

Rocks for Your Axolotl

Add a touch of elegance to your landscape with an array of landscaping stone materials, from river stones, to dragon stone.

Always, the rocks used should contain free of metal and calcium to stop the leaching of metal into your tank.

In the event of doubt the answer is yes, but it's better to stay with store-bought!

Axolotl Hideouts

There are many natural-looking hides available that can be used for a secure haven for your Axolotl in the course of the daytime.

Take into consideration Cichlid rocks, ceramic pipes and Pleco breeding caves for a variety of options.

Axolotl Tank Companions

Do you want to be keeping your Axolotl on its own or could certain tankmates also be used?

It's tempting to fill your tank with all kinds of fish species (after all, the greater the more, right?).

If you want to keep Axies isn't an choice.

There are two motives for conserving these salamanders in one-species habitats:

* Axolotl Threat Axies are highly at risk.

In particular their delicate, external gills can be damaged in calm fish species.

A potential risk for tankmates. As explained more in detail in the next paragraph, Axolotls are carnivores.

In turn, they can be a danger to tankmates, such as schools of fish.

Though they might seem slow while relaxing, you'll be amazed at the speed with which they'll snap at unaware predators!

Some aquarists maintain their Axies with smaller species like guppies or minnows However, they know that the tankmates of these species will likely be consumed sooner or later.

Maintaining a Colony of Axolotls

When you've established that tank mates cannot be found within the Axolotl tank, it is possible that you could be wondering whether it's possible to keep a number of Axolotls with each other.

Yes and no, but it's not a straightforward"yes.

In order to successfully mix Axies, you'll have to take into consideration a variety of aspects.

In the beginning, as we have earlier stated, it is important to be aware of the size of your tank when you are storing many Axolotls.

Because the salamanders are able to grow massive and every one requires their own area, you should ensure that you add 10 gallons to each Axie.

A lack of space could lead to fights where limbs are often lost, and weaker animals could die.

This is especially the case when you mix younger Axolotls or Axolotls that are of different sizes, either of which shouldn't be tried.

Be cautious, make sure that your Axie is equipped with at least one place to hide as well as be sure to monitor the quality of your water.

water's superiority.

What Food Do Axolotls Consume?

Axolotls are predators in the wild, and they will devour anything that moves or is too close Think of aquatic insects, smaller fish, worms. insects that have dropped into the lake, smaller amphibians, even their eggs, and even smaller Axolotls (which occurs quite often).

Which Foods to Avoid When Feeding an Axolotl

In deciding what you feed the Axolotl at the aquarium, there's a few things to take into consideration.

While they're carnivores, these salamanders do not function as an apex predator. They are extremely clumsy, and can be easily wounded by predators that are more aggressive.

Although their stomachs are capable of handling a large quantity, their extremely brittle exoskeletons may cause impaction.

Axolotl guides and other books have used to recommend warm-blooded animal products like liver or beefheart as a good choice for food however, hobbyists do not advocate them.

Also, stay clear of popular feeder goldfish because they do not have the necessary nutrients for the Axies' growth.

Below is a short listing of the foods you should avoid:

* Anything with a tough exoskeleton. Beef heart and the liver (or like fish)

What Kind of Food Should I Feed an Axolotl?

There are a number of top-quality carnivore pellets that can be used to feed Axolotls If you are able to obtain them to eat they are a fantastic everyday food source.

It's the exact issue that not all Axies love pellets.

What other alternatives are you left with?

Worms are considered by many as one of the most nutritious Axolotl products to be found.

This comprises frozen worms like bloodworms, worms that are home-grown such as blackworms, (particularly) earthworms.

This one has a very low fat content, and also a very high nutritional value, particularly when it is gut-loaded using the high-nutrient pellets we mentioned earlier.

Furthermore, worms lack an exoskeleton that is tough and durable as well as the capability to damage the Axolotl.

Cut up the larger worms to prevent any complications. Additionally, they're a fantastic source of protein for Axie.

In addition to pellets and worms In addition, give live guppies and minnows (home-bred to keep away diseases and parasites) tiny insects or even raw fish like codfish.

Eliminate Any Uneaten Food for Axolotls

Keep in mind that Axolotls are very messy eaters that will frequently ignore food items that are right within their reach, avoid food that isn't moving and seems to be alive. They also scatter pieces of food throughout the aquarium.

Be sure to remove food that has been left unattended in a matter of a few hours, in order to ensure the quality of your water!

Food that is not eaten within the tank could cause a range of issues with water quality (which is something is something you should definitely avoid).

Troubleshooting Axolotl Issues

Problems can be encountered at any time in the aquarium hobby. Axolotls do not differ.

In this article, we'll look at a few issues that are frequently covered. concerns.

My Axolotl Is Excessively Hot

In the section on the value of water, Axolotls are not tropical animals and cannot thrive even in extreme heat.

A stressed Axolotl that has been heated will show the white mucus patches that are evident on the forehead.

In addition, it could re-inject food particles or stop eating altogether.

When you discover that an Axolotl is overheated it is the one thing you have to do is slowly return the temperature to the safe range, sit to see if there's no permanent harm.

The best option is to prevent excessive heat in the first place.

Take note of whether the space that you intend to set up your Axie tank is hot during the heat of summer. If it is necessary pick a room that is cooler.

In summer you can use cooling fans or air stones. You may also consider installing an aquarium chilling device or air conditioning system for cooling the space to a lower level.

In the event of extreme heat there may be a need to include ice cubes or water bottles that have been frozen in the tank for help in the enduring of a long temperature wave.

Make sure you've got an accurate thermometer in order to stop your tank from getting too cold!

Aggression Against Axolotls and Limb Loss

Axolotls are predators that don't have any preferences about their prey.

A friend's legs or tails could resemble the taste of a worm. with overcrowding, or grouping juveniles, the salamanders might be bitten by each other.

As injuries could be deadly, it's obvious that staying clear of these scenarios is the most effective option.

In the event of losing or damaged limbs which don't appear to pose a threat to life the most effective option is to isolate the Axolotl and ensure a excellent water quality inside the quarantine tank until injury is healed.

Axolotls have the ability to regenerate body parts like their tail, legs and gills. This implies that an injury-free specimen will usually be fine.

The new legs will likely not appear as attractive as its old ones but they'll let it to function normal.

If you're Axolotl was badly injured by any of the tankmates, visit a veterinarian right away.

There are a few veterinarians who aren't experienced with animals that swim So, make sure you find one and get the contact details of their office prior to purchasing the Axie.

If your veterinarian is unable to treat the wounded Axolotl right away, put it in a tub inside the fridge to reduce the rate of metabolism to wait until it is scheduled.

Axolotl Compaction

In the subsection on substrate Axolotls can be prone to eating tiny rocks and gravel and this can lead to compaction.

In addition, compaction may occur when the Axolotl feeds on insects with hard exoskeletons, which can cause digestive problems. to absorb.

What options do you have when you experience compacting?

The most effective method is to put the affected Axolotl inside the refrigerator (surprising to me, I know...but take it easy).

The metabolism slows and causes the body to work to get rid of all food remaining as fast as it is possible.

This could be advantageous by clearing the system.

After a few days you will begin to notice poop inside the container. If it doesn't it is time to make an appointment with a vet to find out what needs to be taken care of.

Axolotls: Can They Live on Land?

While Axolotls are Neotenic (they don't metamorphose generally) however, the change can happen.

The previously mentioned Axolotl is likely to lose fins and gills.

Eyes bulge, and they develop eyelids. It transforms from a totally aquatic species to one that dwells on the land and breathes air.

The requirements for care are similar to similar to those for the terrestrial tiger salamander. It is a well-known species of amphibian enthusiast.

What's the problem regarding Axolotls who have changed form?

If this shouldn't be expected to occur, what is the reason we have this happening occasionally?

Rarely in very rare instances, an Axolotl can undergo a natural metamorphosis.

Most of the time, however, this procedure occurs because of hormone treatment or circumstances that are horrible that the Axie will become a land-based dweller in order to get away from.

Chapter 4: Ultimate Guide To Keeping And Caring For Axolotl As A Pet

Should we Keep an Axolotl as a Pet?

In certain states, such as California, Maine, New Jersey in some states, including New Jersey, California, Maine and Virginia in some states, it's illegal to possess an axolotl.

It is legal to possess within New Mexico but illegal to import from other states.

Find out your state's exotic pet law to find out if you can keep a pet.

Axolotls originate from Mexico and are considered severely endangered because of destruction of habitats, declining the quality of water, and the urbanization process.

Therefore it is recommended that they not be removed from their natural environment for pets.

The majority of pet axolotls descendants of breeds that were created in captivity for research purposes.

Obtaining Your Axolotl

Be sure to purchase a pet from a reliable breeder or rescue group.

Avoid buying an axolotl through the web or in an advertisement in a classified section or a classified ad unless you talk directly to the vendor and they are able to offer you accurate details about the animal.

If they're not able to give you complete information regarding the origin of the product and history of health, that is an indication of a problem.

Furthermore, it's advisable to talk with people who bought animals from this seller in order to identify the concerns.

A local exotic veterinarian may suggest a trustworthy breeder, or rescue.

Expect to be paying between $20-$70.

The rarer-colored animals like copper generally cost more.

An axolotl that is healthy will be active and can eat as long as it is presented to it.

The skin shouldn't be smooth, nor its body ought to be bulky (as instead of being overweight) but not swelling excessively.

Axolotl Diet

Axolotls are carnivores that require the consumption of meat as a major component.

It is recommended to feed them live crickets and frozen bloodworms, as well as Axolotl pellets.

The ideal is to feed them diverse diets, but they may be a bit finicky in certain instances.

Sometimes Live feeder fish may be fed and are a great source of energy and nutrients.

Axolotls are best fed by hand using tongs or large Tweezers in order to reduce the amount of food wasted and to prevent food from being thrown away within the tank.

It is recommended to feed them twice every week, but preferably in the evening to allow for their night-time habits.

Since axolotls consume their food in whole, it's crucial to feed them with bite-sized portions.

Are You Aware?

Axolotls are neotonic. This means that they live the rest of their existence as larvae and yet reproduce and give offspring.

Axolotls represent the stage of the Salamander's larva, making an amphibian and not the fish.

Axolotls can cause range of health issues.

Infections due to Fungi:

In the absence of scales in Axolotls They are more susceptible to cutting themselves when they touch rough surfaces in the tank.

When food that has been re-gurgitated or not eaten (particularly the meat product) is stored in the tank, and it comes into contact with the Axolotl and a fungal infection may result.

Flags with the color red

Do you notice that your Axolotl display any of the symptoms of illness or disease?

If yes, then please call your vet.

* The development of a film that is white on the body, tail or (treat using 'Pimafix', or an anti-fungal medication)

A less 'fluffy' look on the inside of the gills (check the quality of water)

Availability of Axolotl

Axolotls are often available to purchase through private breeders typically via the Internet.

Because of their incompatibility most reptile-friendly temperatures They are not typically found in reptile shops and at reptile shows.

Although some vendors may have the ability to get them on your behalf but the most reliable sources for healthy axolotls tend to be others who are hobbyists.

Leucistic Axolotls are mostly white, with dark eyes. They often have a few black marks on the top of their bodies.

Axolotl Dimensions

The majority of axolotls have the length of 10 inches (from the point of the nose until the tip of the tail).

There are a few that exceed 12 inches in length, however it is extremely uncommon.

I came across and snapped an 17-inch axolotl which had been seen in order in order to believe it, however these animals are very rare.

At 8 inches long when they attain sexual maturity.

The process can take just six months. However, it usually will take about a year to get good treatment.

Axolotl Life Expectancy

Even though axolotls are known to live past 20 years old, it's rare to meet individuals older than ten years old.

Housing for Axolotls

One adult axolotl may be housed in a 10-gallon reptile fish tank. However, due to the quantity of waste generated by these creatures that are messy an aquarium of 20 gallons is the best option.

In light of the fact that the axolotls are not able to come out of the waters, the land could be discarded.

You can fill the aquarium up to the preferred depth. It will be much easier to keep appropriate water parameters when the aquarium is stocked to the max the same way it is for fish in aquariums.

Always it is recommended to have a lid or an aquarium hood must be on the premises since axolotls are often seen leaping out of their tanks.

Filters can assist in making sure that parameters of the water remain in good condition.

External canister filters, like the Zoo Med Turtle Clean Canister filter are the most suitable choice however, make sure that the aquarium's outlet for water is fitted with the spray bar or any other outlets that spread the flow.

It is because Axolotls are not fish and can't handle distinct water flows.

Axolotls that stay for a prolonged period in areas that have visible water flow can become in a state of hunger and will develop stress-related ailments.

Insomnia and curly Gills can be a sign of strain caused by high volume of water.

Axolotl Temperature and Lighting

Like the majority of amphibians don't require light, even though new species of axolotls are likely to be shy when placed in a bright light but they are able to adjust if they are provided with hidden areas (the typical aquarium "furniture" such as caves as well as wood, vegetation, etc.).

The majority of the time, lighting is employed to improve our enjoyment of watching and also to improve the overall health of aquarium animals and plants.

Pick a bulb appropriate for your plants for example, like the ones used for freshwater aquarium fish.

Keep in mind that light fixtures often generate high temperatures and can be dangerous to Axolotls.

Axolotls are tolerant of temperatures as high as to 70-degrees Celsius.

The mid-to-low 60s are the perfect temperature region.

temperatures of more than 74 degrees Fahrenheit will always cause the exhaustion of heat, hunger loss, and eventually death.

If you're not able to keep temperatures under that level all entire year, then axolotls may not be the right pet in your situation.

If you must own an axolotl and you are concerned about issues with temperature, you might want to consider buying an aquarium chiller to use during the more humid months.

Substrate for Axolotl

Axolotls thrive on aquarium-safe sand, such as Aqua Terra's Aquarium & Terrarium Sand.

If mouth-sized and gravelly objects are readily available and axolotls can be found, they have a terrible practice of eating them.

The result could be stomach trauma and Axolotl's demise.

If you have to make use of gravel, you should consider big pebbles like Exo Terra's Large Natural Turtle Pebbles instead.

Anything less than the size of an axolotl's head can be eaten!

The Salamander's substrate isn't required Salamander substrate is not required. Axolotls don't require it.

A lot of keepers don't use even a single substrate However, a substrate is definitely more pleasing to the eyes in an aquarium that is displayed, and it helps maintain water parameters through providing an area of surface that is suitable for beneficial bacteria.

Axolotl Foods Appropriate staple foods for axolotls comprise living reptile foods like nightcrawlers (large earthworms) and bloodworm cubes frozen bought at pet stores.

Axolotls love frozen shrimp purchased in the market (cooked) and as well as cuts of lean chicken and beef.

Beware of live fish like feeder fish in order to prevent transmission of disease and parasites Axolotls can be susceptible to many parasites and diseases of fish.

Pinkie mice, as well as other fat food items should only be consumed sparingly and should not be used to treat the axolotls.

Similar to most salamanders axolotls are not in need of vitamin or mineral supplementation. It would be difficult to give to animals that swim.

Axolotls are exclusively fed by nightcrawlers, according to my experience, do not develop mineral deficiencies or vitamins.

Water and Axolotl Quality

Tap water can be used to use for axolotls provided it is treated with an aquarium conditioner that can get rid of chloramines and chlorine.

Axolotls tend to be more accepting in the face of low water quality than fish in aquariums, however an effective filter as well as regular change of water is still a must.

If you've owned aquarium fish in the past, this process is likely to be familiar.

The ideal situation is that a fresh aquarium with a filter is run for a period of time before adding axolotls. This will let the conditions in the water to improve and for the bacteria in the filter to grow.

Keep an eye on the parameters of your water by buying water test kits from the aquarium store.

Axolotls are almost without bones inside their bodies, particularly in the early stages of their lives.

The skeleton of their bodies is composed mainly of cartilage.

Axolotls are delicate, small amphibians that have skin permeable.

Therefore, unless required, axolotls shouldn't be handled (they are difficult to catch with the trap of a net).

If you are required to employ a net in transport of an axolotl avoid using nets made of mesh, which could result in injuries to the fingers of the axolotl.

Utilize a delicate, very fine-mesh net.

Axolotls in their early years are prone to nibble at their tankmates' legs as well as the gills. Therefore, they must be kept close only if they are well-fed and have ample space.

Chapter 5: How Long Do Axolotls Live

Axolotls are a kind of salamander, which lives all of its life submerged.

The magnificent animals start out as egg-like creatures they mature around 1 year old.

They're in danger of becoming extinct in their natural habitat in Mexico City, with populations decreasing daily.

However, they are much more sought-after exotic pets than they ever were and there are more in captivity, compared to the wild.

The axolotl's life span stage, as well as what they are compared to salamanders.

Axolotls: How Long Do They Live?

Axolotls usually live between 10 and 15 years in captivity. They could live as long as 20 years if they are properly cared for.

The oldest known axolotl has not been identified however their age could amaze you as they grow more loved as pets thanks to the long-lasting nature of certain salamander species (more on that later!)

While the axolotl can be described as one of the salamanders that live only a few days due to their small size, they can live for longer than the majority of people imagine in the event that they decide to adopt them as pets!

They are able to withstand the rigors of life due to the ability of them to regenerate the body's parts, such as organs and limbs!

The life span of an Axolotl in captivity vs. when it is in the Wild

Axolotls are kept in captivity for around 10 to 15 years. They live in the wild for around 5-10 years.

What are the factors that contribute to this huge gap in the length of life?

In their natural habitats the salamanders are in danger from a variety of dangers like diseases, predators as well as habitat loss.

The reality of being a captive can be challenging.

Like in the case of many exotic pets Axolotls get poor care.

Parents could consider purchasing a pet with the false notion that marine animals can be easily handled.

Furthermore, they are purchased at a moment's notice, like most people would do with smaller pets.

If properly taken care of, an axolotl could live for up to 20 years. This makes adoption an important decision that shouldn't be made at a risk!

Development and Lifecycle of the Axolotl

Axolotls live their whole life in water. They even breeding under water.

In the months of December through June, they can breed. Females are able to lay as many as 1000 eggs during the same year!

Axolotls are kept inside a jellylike substance following the hatching.

Before entering the larval stage, they'll begin to grow their head and build a body.

Axolotl larvae are clear and they do not grow legs until about two weeks into the larval stage.

The stage is maintained until they attain sexual maturity and they are capable of breeding when they reach six months old.

When they reach the age of one the axolotls are believed to be mature.

What are the Most Common Axolotl Death Causes?

A white axolotl swims in the water, surrounded by lush Reeds

Predators

Axolotls do not have self-defense capabilities.

They are slow to move and do not have teeth or claws.

These are the easiest prey for predators in the wild.

Axolotls have been also targeted by the invasive species that have invaded their habitats.

Pollution Environmental pollution axolotl population has been wiped out due to their tiny native habitat near the lakes close to Mexico City.

The species was close to extinction because of the pollution of water, and is endangered in the wild in the present.

Health Concerns

Axolotls have a tendency to develop illnesses that can cause swelling of the fluids, tumors bacteria, fungi, as well as parasites.

Axolotls are afflicted with a range of health issues that are due to breeding.

Sadly the gene pool of their species is decreasing as they near their extinction on the open seas.

A variety of conditions can be triggered from poor maintenance, such as the inability to filter water within the tank, water that is dirty, or injuries resulting from poor tanks' setup or handling.

Insufficient Care

In captivity, insufficient medical care could lead to loss of an axolotl that is delicate.

Although they're more adaptable than the majority of species of fish, they require certain requirements for cooling water, a huge tank and a proper substrate that is located at the top of the tank.

Do your own investigation prior to acquiring an animal, and do not depend on stores selling pets to advise you on what's most suitable.

Most of the time, they are only focused on the sale of the animal and not the aftermath of adoption.

Axolotls shouldn't be handled or taken out of the water because of their fragile bodies and limbs and their slimy coat.

The thin coat of slime acts as a protection against parasites and bacteria.

The axolotl can be removed using your hands or dried when the axolotl has been removed from the water. So they're much more of a glance and don't play kind of animal!

In the end, axolotls have been known to jump from tanks.

The lid must be used to ensure they are alive and inside the fresh water.

What is the Axolotl's Life Expectancy in Relation to Other Salamanders?

A Japanese huge salamander. Notice how big they are in comparison to the axolotls.

The salamanders that live longest are known to reach 52 years old.

At the Amsterdam Zoo, they were Japanese huge salamanders.

There are stories that Chinese giant salamanders aging more than 200 years old However, with no additional details about the life span of this giant salamander is not known.

Chapter 6: Fascinating Axolotl Facts

Axolotls (pronounced"a*suh*laa*tls) are salamanders that live in water in the wild in only the Mexico City area's Lake Xochimilco.

Because of their capability to grow organs, these threatened amphibians also enjoy popularity for their pets. They are also breed in captivity for studies in the field of science.

The destruction of habitats and the spread of species that are invasive have caused a significant reduction in the number of Axolotls.

They are small in terms of size and color and maintain their characteristics as larvae through their existence.

Their distinctive look, often featuring sparkling pink skin as well as cute headdresses (which can actually be their Gills) have earned their fans around the world.

Explore the most interesting information about the axolotl including their unique mating routines to their astonishing regeneration capabilities.

1. Axolotls Remain Adorable Throughout Their Lives

Axolotls are neotenic species meaning they achieve sexual maturity, but retain all their characteristics as larvae.

So, even though some amphibians, like salamanders, grow breathing organs and later reside on land, the Axolotls have their distinct gills that are feathery and external, but remain aqua.

It also means the teeth do not develop, and they are required to consume food through suction.

2. They Are Native to a Singular Location on Earth

The habitat that is the native home of axolotl is under threat.

They were located in two lakes at high elevation within Mexico City, but are today found just in one area:

Xochimilco Lake is located in the southern part of Mexico City.

The previous home, Lake Chalco in central Mexico City, was drained in order to stop flooding.

Xochimilco is now the size of a canal, and axolotls are getting increasingly rare due to destruction of habitat and the arrival of predatory carp as well as the tilapia.

3. Themselves Are Carnivores

Axolotls are carnivores that consume many prey items including worms, fish to crustaceans and insects.

They're not selective and they will eat alive or dead animal flesh.

They often eat brine shrimp and strips of beef liver Earthworms, fish pellets while in captive.

Axolotls especially the young as well as those who have a deficient amount of food, can be a victim of acting cannibalistic, and even biting off the appendages from a close family member.

Fortunately, damaged axolotl is able to easily grow back the body part that was injured due the fact that they are able to regenerate.

4. They Are Available in a Range of Color Patterns

Axolotls Color patterning and pigmentation is due to the four genes that make up their genome.

Axolotls generally dark brown to black with olive or gold scattered specks found when they are in their natural habitat.

Like others salamanders, also change color so that they blend into their environment.

Albino or leucistic (with diminished pigmentation) as well as pink axolotls tend to be more prevalent in animals that are bred for captive.

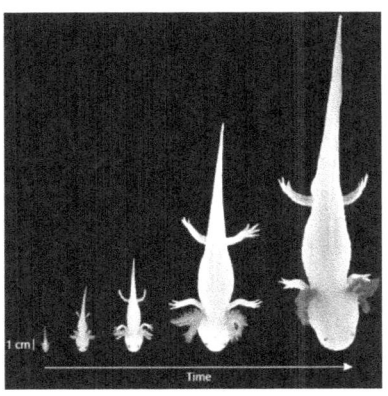

Furthermore, the gills with feathers on the front of the axolotl's head have pigmentation, especially in the vibrant red hue seen in albino Axolotls.

5. They Have the Ability to Regenerate Body Parts

Many amphibians as well as fish can regenerate their tails and limbs Axolotls can take this up a notch by regeneration of jaws, spinal chords skin, tissues from their ovaries and lungs and even fragments of their hearts as well as brains.

Axolotls can also renew itself throughout its lifetime.

The capability of the cell type to regenerate itself is of particular interest scientists who want to bring this technology to humans.

It is a remarkable ability:

"If an axolotl suffers loss of one of its limbs, it will restore it in the right dimensions and direction.

Within a few weeks after that, the line between older and modern disappears completely."

6. They Possess a Massive Genome

The axolotl genome has 32 billion DNA base, and 10 times that of humans, scientists are faced with the daunting task of studying the Axolotl's DNA.

It is vital as it can aid scientists in discovering how axolotl utilizes stem cells to re-create tissues.

Researchers have discovered two genes that are involved within axolotl regeneration.

Axolotls are known for their amazing regenerative capabilities, researchers have widened their studies to cover other organs of the body as well as retina regeneration.

Based on the Smithsonian the Smithsonian, they're "basically the white mice of amphibians" because of their distinctive genetic profile as well as ability to unlock the mysteries of the evolution process and regeneration.

7. Their Relationship

Dancing Is Involved in Rituals

Once axolotls attain six months of age at which point they're ready to be mated.

The sequence begins with adult animals touching their cloacal areas against each other, and it moves on around in a dance-like, circular sequence.

In nature females lay between 100 and 300 eggs, and they breed every year. However, in captivity the breeding process is more frequent.

When the eggs are properly placed, parental involvement removed.

In between 10 and 14 days, the eggs begin to hatch and the new axolotls become self-sufficient.

8. They Face Serious Endangerment

The axolotl, found in only a tiny area of Mexico and is extremely endangered within the natural world.

They cover just under four square miles of ecosystem that is rapidly declining because of development, pollution and the spread of the spread of invasive species.

Their importance to research as well as their capacity to reproduce in captivity could aid in their longevity, though not always in the wild.

Researchers estimated that their number was down by 90 percent in the year 2009.

Chapter 7: Lodging An Axolotl As Expected As Well As Other Facts

Lodging the Axolotl

In any case, a 15 to 20-gallon tank for fish is recommended for Axolotls. Be sure that the tank is equipped with the safety of a top that is secure, since they are known to attempt to climb from their hiding places. The land area isn't necessary to the tank's fully amphibian animals. In the minimum, the water's depth should not be greater than your axolotl. The addition of depth can improve the quality of your water as well as give your pet greater mobility.

Install the tank set in the coolest room away from bright sunlight, with temperatures in between 55 and 68°F (14 or 20 Celsius) Do not allow the temperature to exceed 75°F (24 degree Celsius). There is no need for a special lighting for Axolotls (in contrast to other reptiles). A dull hiding location, like the vase placed on the side, as well as an aquarium is usually appreciated.

Certain owners opt to leave the lower portion of the tank unprotected However, others recognize that it can put stress on the axolotl the event that it doesn't find traction on the base. If rocks are used on the foundation, it ought to be a coarse stone that's larger than the head of the axolotl. The fine rock can be consumed which could cause obstruction.

The water that is treated using an aquarium conditioner which gets rid of chloramines and chlorine perfect for Axolotls. Do not use refined water and make sure that the pH of your water remains within the range of 6.5 to 7.5. (You are able to find the water test kits to test everything at pet stores.) Many owners discover that an aquarium with sifting is easier to manage due to the fact that the water that is not filtered requires regular change to get rid of waste. However it is the case that you choose to install channels in the tank, then the filtration rate should be low. The most amazing channels which create massive flows may pressurize the Axolotl.

In the case of a tank that is separated the cleaning process is usually 20% water changes each week, as well as siphoning the waste from the bottom within the tank. If you're not using channels, then you must do a 20% daily water change or at least every other each day. Don't ever do a total water change as it could alter the water technology too significantly and strain the animal.

The most intriguing facts:

i.They can retrieve appendages, which is what drives scientists to consider their possibilities.

ii.Basically it is the case that an Axolotl is the name given to a fledgling the Lizard. However, unlike the lizards which are fledglings who reside only in water but then change into land creatures, Axolotls don't totally.

In the end, scientists came up with a method to end their experiment by employing some synthetic substances in their research. Since Axolotls should not be considered to be earthly lizards The life expectancy of their species was not long.

Conduct of the Axolotls

Axolotls are also unable to feel the sense of their own space. I've seen scenes where an Axolotl sits on another Axolotl. The Axolotl that is perched on think of anything else and barely notices the extra weight. Also, I've seen my Axolotls use each other to their advantage and use the other Axolotl as a stage for the other to bounce off of.

Chapter 8: An Axolotl Diet As Well As The Known Healthissues Plus Its Legality

Water and food Axolotls in the wild are axolotls that feed on worms, snails as well as scavengers. Little fish, as well as tiny animals of water and land. While in jail, they may be provided with a variety of saltwater shrimp, small pieces of liver or hamburger bloodworms, night crawlers tubifex worms, various frozen varieties of fish food, as well as business fish pellets. Be careful not to manage them using the worms you have caught yourself, since they may carry parasites. In general there is no need for mineral or nutrient supplements are required. Consult your vet as to the amount of the food you can offer as well in regards to the frequency of taking the care of your axolotl because this varies based on size and age. In general, many adults eat a small amount every week. The most effective method to handle this is by putting food with round-nosed forceps near to the animal. It is also possible to put the food down in the tank as close to the axolotl as is likely to be. If you find that your axolotl does not like eating much throughout the day, try taking an attempt at taking control of the situation in the evening, when it's more energetic. Get rid of any uncooked food items out of the tank daily in order to ensure that the water is clear.

Essential Health Problems One remarkable feature of axolotls is their ability to regenerate. Due to wounds that don't really impede their growth their ability to grow, they're able to regenerate their tails, appendages and even other body organs like the eye and heart tissue. However, this amazing capability doesn't prevent their bodies from the ravages of illness. Tank conditions that are unsanitary can cause bacteria or viruses and the signs of which are characterized by a loss of appetite or torpidity. of hunger. Additionally, the odor of chemicals that are derived from waste within the tank could create a harmful odor. If this occurs, you might notice a lack of energy and uncontrollable craving, as well as irritation, panting and achy skin within the creature's body. Axolotls that have rocks in their tanks with enough size for them to consume are more likely to suffer digestive issues. If the axolotl is confronted with a predator the likelihood is that it'll be quiet and won't will want to consume food. In addition, if the issue isn't promptly treated, the death is likely to occur rapidly. Additionally, occasionally change into an earthly form. The reasons behind this can be unclear, but might be due to the chemical or water quality. This transformation could be extremely uncomfortable for an axolotl which can drastically reduce the lifespan of your pet. In the event that you observe strange changes in the body of your pet, like it being able to grow larger, consult an animal veterinarian with practical knowledge of colorful pets examine immediately.

Is It Legal to Own a Pet Axolotl? Axolotls are illegal to possess in certain states like California, Maine, New Jersey and Virginia. The state of New Mexico, they are legally allowed to keep, however they are illegal to import from other states. Make sure you check the local regulations to ensure you are allowed to keep one. Axolotls are native to Mexico and considered threatened species due to environmental mishaps as well as water pollution and the presence of invasive species. Therefore, they should not be taken out of nature for trade of pets. Most pet axolotls come from hostage reproductions of animals that were used as a means of logical investigation.

More on Axolotls' Feeding (More Explanations)

Axolotls can be described as carnivores. They don't have a lot of demands and will eat almost whatever will fit in their mouths.

There are several foods that are considered to be an essential part of the Axolotl diet, as well as other foods that are thought of as bites. Axolotls have the ability to consume:

*earthworms,

*red wigglers,

*brine shrimp,

*daphnia,

* blood worms,

*ghost shrimp and more.

Chapter 9: Buying Your Amazing Axolotl At The Right Time

Buying Your Axolotl

Always purchase a pet from a respected raiser or salvage group. You should not purchase an axolotl on the internet or through an organized promotion, unless the event that you've talked to the vendor and they're able to supply you with accurate information about the animal. If they aren't able to provide you with thorough information about the origins of the creature as well as its health and wellness history, that should be a sign of caution. Also, it is advisable to speak to people who've purchased pets from this vendor to find out if there are any concerns. A nearby vet can often assist you in finding a suitable increaser or salvage.

You can expect to spend somewhere between the region of between $20 and the total figure of $70. Animals with unusual shades, such as copper, generally be more expensive. An axolotl that is solid will be lively, and could take food in the event you give it. Skin should not be flaky and its body needs be fairly strong (instead of being overweight) However, it should not be growing in any way that is unusual.

The accompanying diagram shows the various prices for axolotls based upon their extraordinary quality.

-White Albino Axolotl$20 to $40

-Wild Type Axolotl$20 to $30

-Green Florescent Protein Axolotl~$70

-Lucy Axolotl$28 to $35

-Gold Albino Axolotl$25 to $35

-Copper Axolotl~$85

Uncommon AxolotlsBased on Sellers.

Chapter 10: The Correct Tanks For Your Axolotl And Other Facts

The Correct Tank for an Axolotl

In relation to choosing the right tank, there are a myriad of different nuances that must be observed. Take into consideration every aspect. What amounts of furnishings, foods and other things do we carry about? The answer is a huge amount, doesn't it?

In fact, the axolotl won't need to worry about that whole amount to be examined, but there are some things he should be doing to stay engaged.

Size

Axolotls require at the very least an aquarium that holds at least ten gallon. The best size for tanks is 20 gallons however. There is a reason for this, which is Axolotls are able to produce more waste than fish could, and they're higher than most fish in general in that the abundance of garbage will refill the tank quickly, so larger the tank, the lesser chance you'll have to sift out the dung.

The size of the tank gives the axolotl to have more opportunities. At the very least, if you take a look at essentials again, you'll need to fill up the tank enough to completely cover the axolotl its own chance of success which it had all the way. The majority of the time, it would be about 10 crawls or a foot water. But, I always provide my Axolotl approximately a substantial amount of space to give him plenty of room to move around.

If the tank that you use for your axel is shared with other axolotls, then there will be a need for the size of your tank to increase by 20 gallons each one axolotl. It should provide them with lots of space, with their own space in the chance they wish.

Rock

The material or rock is used to cover the bottom of your tank are crucial. Two options are available to make sure you choose a quality substance like sand which will be used for a substrate, or the rocks are huge and used for a variety of rocks.

The issue with small stones is they Axolotls are known to eat small stones which can impede the stomach-related poop. It is extremely dangerous for the axolotl. It could result in some of one of the most well-known health issues in the axolotl. Beware of the stones in these set.

Some groups do not to use rock or even substrate. Although this may be desirable, in comparison to using small stones, it is the only circumstance where it's desirable the absence of a ground surface inside tanks.

Axolotls require the deck to possess some grip to slide through the earth.

In the event that there is just the lower glass part in the tank it can confuse and trouble the Axolotl. In order to avoid this, make sure you add stones or substrate to aid in the development of the Axolotl.

Channel

We will then look at the channel. Every animal that is tank bound will need a good channel. If there's no channel then you'll have to clean the tank of water manually and that will mean a lot of supplanting tanks of your axolotl. The process becomes dull, and easily prevented by using the help of a channel.

Channels may price, but there are channels available priced at just $15 or $165. Another type of channel that to consider is the corner or crate channel.

Chapter 11: Axolotls And Suitable Tankmates, Plus Other Facts

Axolotls work best when mixed with other Axolotls. The best situation for Axolotls is an animal-friendly group that is tank-only, but in this case, there's the one fundamental principal.

Do not keep teenagers in a group. It is best to separate them once they have their first legs. Axolotls smaller than six inches (15 centimeters) have the barbarian stage, and could bite or chew off body parts of their tankmates.

In the event that you're planning to add an additional Axolotl into your aquarium, make sure to keep them out of your tank. A handful of Axolotls could be real wild animals.

Fish

Axolotls have the ability and are willing to consume anything that fits in their mouth. So, whatever fish is eaten. This is it.

However, you wouldn't wish to keep these fish along with those with a massive, powerful size. Certain species might appreciate nibbling off the frilly gills of the Axolotls but they could also hurt the fish. The feeder fish recommended for Axolotls are the sole fish I'd recommend.

Bantam Shrimp

Bantam shrimp (for example, Ghost shrimp) can be put in the tank along with Axolotls. The shrimp could frighten the Axolotls at first. The appearance shrimp can be a nibble to the Axolotls. So, don't think they'll be long haul tank buddies. They can be a good occasionally-take but.

Snails

Do not keep Axolotls in a room with freshwater snails as well. They'll try to eat them, and this could affect the axolotl killing the Axolotl. Anything smaller than the head should not be put into the tank. Be aware that anything moving could be prey for predators, and so snails can be described as an incredibly slow, massive "worm" for them.

A small number of groups believe that there is a need to protect Pond snails as well as Bladder snails should be axolotl secured since their shells aren't a threat to the Axolotl. In reality, I wouldn't recommend anyone to try this.

African Dwarf Frogs

Incredibly, I've come across numerous inquiries regarding gatherings with regards to the similarity between African Dwarf Frogs, and Axolotls. It's not possible to keep these two animals together due to of two main reasons:

i.As you the moment speculated that Axolotls may try to eat tiny African Dwarf Frog.

ii. African Dwarf Frogs require extremely hot temperatures in their tanks.

Handling Axolotls

Many people ask if I be able to reach them? Could I engage with them, or obtain their attention?

In short, no. Axolotls are totally sea-going creatures. They never be able to leave the water for any time throughout their lives. This means that they aren't available for purchase as pets that you could enjoy with. In essence, they can't survive without water for time.

However, in the unlikely occasion that you must transfer them from one tank and then move to the following, you can use a slender net and cover the gap to ensure Axolotl does not escape.

Do not touch their hands, unless when there's no other option. If this is the case you should make sure they are completely dry and perfect. Wash your hands thoroughly. Keep in mind that any buildup on the hands (even cleansing products) Axolotl will assimilate through the skin.

They also have an ooze coat, which is prone to being damaged by unintentional contact. The best option is use gloves. The majority of people don't like it too much, so I'd keep contact to an absolute at.

In the previous chapters Axolotls can be owned as pets. However, their plight is not safe. Axolotls prohibited to be claimed or transfer to specific states. The majority of states allow Axolotls However, there are handful of exemptions. You must determine whether Axolotls can be claimed within your state before purchasing the Axolotls.

Chapter 12: Water Alteration/Maintenance, Axolotl Sexing As Well As Some Likely Challenges Of The Axolotls

Water Changes as Well as Maintenance

Axolotls are messy animals that create a large amount of garbage. They are garbage machines. Therefore, it's crucial to get rid of it as soon as you spot it. In the event that you fail to do this immediately it is possible that it are going to remain there and spread everywhere.

TIP: It's essential to conduct week-by- weekly water adjustments to ensure your level in the right place. 1/3 of the water needs be removed week after week, and replaced with fresh chlorine-free water.

Sexing Axolotls

Axolotls have a lot of duration to frame their intimate parts in a proper manner. You may think that an Axolotl female could become a male once their body has been formed correctly. There is no way to tell for sure which gender is an Axolotl when they're an entire year older.

According to the study according to the investigation, adult Axolotls begin sexual development from the age of 10 to a one year and half. As axolotls begin to develop their fingers will start changing their tone. At this point, that you will be able to determine the gender of the Axolotls. Axolotls with lighter hues can result in dark fingers, while more obscure colored axolotls can produce lighter-colored fingers.

Axolotl Privates are straight even with their sane legs under their tails. Males may have a large the cloaca. This is similar to the round knock. Females could have an unbalanced opening, however they don't have a bulging Cloaca.

There is a chance that you will discover that what you believed to be a female has turned out to be a man after you notice they've put together a massive knock despite not having a knock at all by any way. Females also grow to be more powerful than men. The guys will generally have more length and be smaller.

In the case of is about my Axolotls it is possible to see in the undisputed sexual orientation differences. When you examine the pictures, you will see that males have an enormous knock, while the female is almost without knock, so it is easy to observe the difference between these two types of genital.

The female's size is also huge when compared to males. It is due to the fact that females have the capacity to produce eggs, whereas males make sperm for the preparation of eggs. The idea of presenting two genders that are opposite and specifically forming Axolotls fascinatingly, could enable mating.

Rearing Axolotls

Axolotl men will give the spermatophores. They are referred to as the sperm cones. They look like an acceptable jam like substance, and men can transport these all over the tank. Some guys might try to place females on sperm cones, which could be akin to an unusual dancing.

A daily romantic schedule for males and females occurs where the two be able to connect while they dance the "waltz."

If the male is successful, the female will begin to lay eggs in the tank quickly or within a few days. Females are prone to acting extremely hysterical, which is quite unusual from the species. Axolotls tend to not be seen moving around during the suppertime. It is common to see females running around the tank looking for a suitable spot to lay eggs. The eggs will be laid in the open areas of plants and other surfaces.

Axolotls have the capacity to lay as many as 1000 eggs. If you're not ready to breed your own Axolotls be sure to keep males and females separate! Otherwise, you could end in a big pile of eggs that are growing with soundness that can in the future produce.

Certain eggs will not hatch on the off possibility that they're too unpractical. Many reproduction companies sell eggs in solid form prior to incubation or break them into plastic containers until they are old enough to be able to ship or transport to the new owners.

Potential Problems Related to Axolotls

Nipping:

The nipping or gnawing of a pet can cause the cause of conflict between Axolotls. In the event that there's not enough food available or there isn't enough space within a tank, then Axolotls could nip each other. By providing enough food and hiding places will keeps your Axolotls active and in normal, laidback creatures.

Personally, I prefer to care for my Axolotls on their own so that they do not struggle over falling food. I stay by till they're at the independent closings of the tank. Then, I drop food from each end. It's not necessary to do this, but it's an option to limit fighting when you are unsure of your Axolotls are generally fighting with food.

Incorporating other species into the tank using the help of an Axolotl that was described previously, could be unwise due to the fact that a variety of species prefer to nibble on Axolotl Gills. Axolotls are able to recover appendages However, it's best to keep the risk of a threat at a minimum whatever could be anticipated.

Be aware that substrates made of rock like those the ones you can see in aquariums can be extremely dangerous for this species.

Home Pets:

Other pets can also be potential problems with Axolotls. Felines are now prone to in smacking Axolotls from the tank or become curious about tank's the water. Tank tops are a great option to families that have pets of different breeds they can also keep Axolotls away from leaping off the tank, which is a surprise.

Chapter 13: More On Axolotl Care, Regeneration Plus Other Amazing Infomation

Axolotls have been adapted to an specific climate, and can't be completely adaptable to different climates. It is essential to maintain your tank in the temperature that axolotl prefers, or probably, your tank will be pressured or injuries.

Whatever the case may be, axolotls' demeanours are likely to be the most amazing thing you can find in any animal. They're intelligent and don't require much maintenance apart from cleaning the tank and cleaning.

Consider an axolotl, on the off chance you're prepared to establish a environment for it, and you require the animal to make you smile.

To get a deeper in-depth and thorough understanding of each of the areas worth examining, it is recommended to concentrate on an axolotl glance at this extensive consideration management.

Appendage R e-growth

When Axolotls come up in discussions There are two aspects which usually come up during the discussion the charming smile or yawn, and their amazing capacity for regenerative. Regenerative potential of axolotls is extremely complex and stunningly awesome.

What can an Axolotl's regeneration react?

What about looking at the things an axolotl is able to be able to recover.

Here's a small selection of the most crucial recuperation achievements.

*Limbs

*Brain

*Jaw

*Spine

*Heart

In the moment that I was able to say almost everything, I wouldn't make fun of this. The wounds are closed quickly and they are each filled in like they hadn't suffered any injuries in any way.

Does there exist a time limit to what frequency this occurs However, what is the cut-off? Do axolotls simply extend their arms repeatedly? This is similar to the nine lives of felines as they are known to have right? It's not true.

The cord, squeeze it, remove a part which will then be regenerated. It is possible to cut off the appendages on any level such as the wrist, elbow, and the upper arm. It will be able to recover. It's optimal.

The procedure isn't too complicated to worry about, and there's not any scarring around the location of removal. each of the tissues is replaced. It is possible to recover the same appendage 50, 60 or 100 times. Furthermore, they can do it without failing: fantastic.

What is the best way to describe the size of the structure? Do you think it takes an extended period of time for these amazing animals to grow their appendages?

In general, it can take between 40 and 50 days for the regrowth of an appendage. The time could be longer due to due to the size of the appendage that it requires to grow. When axolotls become more experienced and mature, their size increases. The process of regaining the appendage takes longer. However it is a constant process to returned to its appropriate dimensions for the body of an axolotl.

How Does an Axolotl's Regeneration Work?

Regenerative interactions are incredibly complicated, so I'm inconceivably distortionizing it here. However in a quick sketch:

A wound can be created.

*The epidermal cells in that area create an epidermis injury.

*Injured epidermis cells duplicate that frame the blastema.

*The blastema gets straightened and expands until it is the correct dimension.

The appendage becomes unclear and is not distinct from the body.

The first stage is the one that occurs at the moment of injury, nearly none of the blood flow is taken because the body of the axolotl gets pushed quickly into its healing process.

Stage 2: Cells all over the body are transformed into nondifferentiated cells, and then form the epidermis of an injury.

Stage 3: These cells begin rapidly increasing, levels where blastema gets being framed. It is a cone-shaped collection of cells that are not differentiated.

Stage 4: The duplicated cells expand to match the dimension of the axolotl's body as it straightens from the cone-like structure that it began in.

In the fifth stage, the differentiated cells transform into the cells that they were and the appendages work in unison.

What is the reason why Axolotl Regeneration so important? Let's imagine we can equip the regenerative power from the axolotl. Patients with amputated legs, casualties from eating or even malignant tumor sufferers could have their pain removed from them. The study of axolotl's disease and their recuperation is based on this reason. For clarity, this isn't just a flurry of investigations that researchers are currently examining. It is important to realize that axolotls are regarded as the oldest recorded laboratory animals. It is due to their nonchalant nature, however also in light of the myriad of secrets that remain to be disclosed about the axolotl's recuperation.

The study of axolotls successfully produced a number of results by way of attempting to unravel the genome of an axolotl, we found an unbreakable connection between the macrophages that make up an axolotl's resilient frame and the capacity of its regenerative.

The cause was revealed by the researchers who smothered macrophages within the axolotl, and it could not develop back appendages which were removed. When they were done it was that they formed scar tissue in the area, similar to how the human's wound heals.

Chapter 14: Axolotls Are Commonly Referred

Axolotls are amphibians that live in the land. axolotl is an amphibian particularly a salamander that doesn't undergo metamorphosis in its natural form. When they are young, amphibians usually are characterized by gills, and they live in water. As adults, they shed the gills and acquire lungs and live on the land.

Adult Axolotls keep their gills intact and live on in water. Gills are the most distinct feature because they look like feathers.

Axolotls also have lungs. While their main method of breathing is through their gills, they also make use of their lungs in order to draw air out of the surface of the water. Since they live their entire life in waters, they possess feet with webbed legs and tails to swim.

Axolotls are adorable and are great pets.

If you're looking for an animal with a distinct look then the axolotl that has its distinctive and awkward nature is the thing you're looking for.

Axolotls are simple to care for and do not require any special equipment. They do require a specific habitat to thrive.

This Book will provide you with the essentials of a simple-to-maintain tank, and also how to give the proper treatment it requires to thrive.

Axolotls reside in aquariums, and are thriving in waters that are either cold or room temperature and have minimal light. If everyone had 10 liters water in their tank, they could live in peaceful smaller groups.

In addition to a reliable aquarium pump You don't require additional equipment for caring for the axolotls. Because of their sensitive to the conditions of water, however the tank requires frequent cycle and maintenance.

The scientific name is Ambystoma mexicanum

* Species: A. mexicanum

*The Ambystomatidae family

* The name of the genus is Ambystoma

* Length: 6-18 inches

* Time: between 10 and 15 years

Axolotl (Ambystoma mexicanum) history goes back hundreds of years prior in the Aztec culture of Mexico. The amphibians' names are for Xolotl which is the Aztec divinity of death believed to have changed into an axolotl to not be killed.

It was in 1863 that axolotls became the first animals to come into Europe. For studies on the development of the limb A group of 34 animals were brought to Lake Xochimilco in Mexico to France. In their lives as pets, they quickly expanded across Europe as well as the overwhelming majority of axolotls that are captive-bred around the world be traced at least a small portion of their ancestry back to the research group that originally started it all.

Many lovers of amphibians and fish keep axolotls as pets due to their captivating nature, charming features, and their huge dimensions. But, they can live more than one foot. Additionally, their life span is fifteen years. They are a significant expenditure in time as well as space.

Axolotls are usually sedentary animals that love to lie in the bottom of tanks. Their habit of laying down has earned them the title "walking fish." An individual can be housed in a 15 gallon large fish tank, which has at minimum six inches of water space.

The salamanders that are in question are predators that can be fierce. They'll try to devour everything smaller than them when they are in nature. It is not recommended to keep them with amphibians and fish due to the fact that they are omnivores. The live prey, which includes bloodworms, earthworms, and blackworms, are eaten by Axolotls. Some pet species have been that have been reported to eat meat heart pieces raw fish and frozen-thawed Mysis shrimp, as well as brine shrimp.

When properly taken care of An axolotl can live longer than 10 years. They can provide any lucky caretaker with a fascinating look into the past of Salamanders. They're certainly among the most rare pets.

This species is prone to stress and need to be handled with care. The species can be stressed due to handling, bright lights and high temperatures. It also suffers from poor conditions of the water and strong flow. Axolotl, Mexican walking fish as well as Mexican Salamander are some of its most popular name.

A mature axolotl could be between 8-16 inches (15 to 45cm) and is extremely appealing with its big head, eyes without lids, as well as four long, slim legs that have a longer fingers.

Axolotls include rami. They are gill stalks with filaments which protrude out from the back of their necks.

But it's their ability to regenerate themselves that captivates and astonish us. Axolotls are able to regenerate nearly every body part which includes the arm, leg, foot and the brain. Actually they are the Axolotl is the largest human genome that has been sequenced to date and has 32 billion pair of base pairs (10x more than human).

Unfortunately, Lake Xochimilco is home to the last remaining wild axolotls that exist in the entire world.

Axolotls are listed in the IUCN's annual Red List of vulnerable species because of their lack of availability.

As Lake Calcho (the axolotl's natural habitat within Mexico) was empty to stop flooding which caused the population to suffer an enormous blow. The result was that huge quantities of axolotls were eradicated as survivors began to populate the canals in Xochimilco. The species is flourishing within the aquarium industry. Axolotls can live about 17 years provided they are given the proper maintenance and care.

Chapter 15: Axolotl Care Sheet And Setup Of Tank

A complete knowledge of tank maintenance, cycle, and water quality is necessary for care at Axolotl.

If you aren't experienced with maintaining your aquarium and water cycles could find it hard to care for an Axolotl. People who are familiar with maintaining fish for pets as well as nitrogen cycling will have no problem maintaining their overall well-being.

The most efficient way to keep the quality of your water is through regular test and use of filters for aquariums. The problem is that most filters do not be able to handle large solids such as uncooked or reconstituted food items. Therefore, food waste must be disposed of out of the tank following each meal as it could result in illness.

Each 2 months, your tank needs to be thoroughly cleaned with the gravel siphon to eliminate any debris filters have missed. Food waste and uncooked or reabsorbed food can also cause high levels of ammonia as well as nitrite. Additionally, the water in an aquarium is required to be checked regularly with tests for water quality. The optimal pH level is 6.5-7.5 However, a higher value of 6.5 is preferable.

Axolotls are a cold-water species. Axolotls are accustomed to temperatures of 14-18 degrees Celsius. Because of their skin's delicate, Axolotls should be handled with care and attention is required when nets are used to ensure they don't get caught in. Every part of an Axolotl which is bit off or badly injured could grow in the future, including the tail, and the head.

Prior to bringing your pet's Axolotl in their new aquarium be sure to confirm that nitrogen cycling is complete.

Axolotl Tank Requirements & Setup

In the beginning, you need to select your aquarium. It is possible to keep an axolotl in an aquarium that is 10 gallons however it is easier to manage them within a 20-gallon tank.

Axolotls can produce a great deal of waste. Providing an additional body of water will help keep the balance of conditions of your aquarium. Space for floor should be prioritized over the height.

Two options are available as a substrate for your home: sand or a flat bottom.

Tanks with bare base is straightforward to keep clean and maintained However, if your an axolotl can't grasp the bottom and become anxious, it could be a problem.

Axolotls consume food by drawing water in their mouths. Hence that a surface made up of gravel could be taken in. In the event that this happens this could lead to serious digestive problems, including impaction.

Sand is by far the best option for a safe and secure home to keep Axolotls in your home as pets. Sand particles are tiny and are unlikely to cause to your pet axolotl anything serious when they are ingested. Axolotls enjoy digging, and play in the sand. This could significantly increase their well-being and keep them from being distracted.

Utilize fine sand in order to keep the fish from inhaling gravel that could cause stomach problems. Within the aquarium, rock or driftwood can be used as hiding areas as well as caves. Living plants can be utilized however they should be sturdy and established.

Axolotls are night-time creatures and do not have eyelids to protect them from the harsh sunlight, so they ought to expose themselves to light during 10-12 hours every day, while provided with adequate protection. Because of their rapid growth and rapid growth, the young Axolotls need more oxygen therefore an air-pump should be provided. As they age the metabolism slows down and the oxygen requirements decrease.

It is possible to decorate your aquarium with lots of plant life (java anubias, moss and hornwort are all great choices) and hideouts such caves (can utilize PVC pipes or plant pots).

Axolotls are not obligated to meet light requirements, however they can be agitated when they are exposed to light that is too high in brightness. A better option is to select a low-light LED lamp which allows you to control the intensity and help keep your plants in good health.

In the past, Axolotls may generate a massive amount of trash. It is necessary to have a strong filter, however ensure that it does not cause an excessive flow of water.

Axolotls produce static, or slow-moving water. The use of a spray-bar is to spread the flow, and reduce its impact. The plants can also be utilized to reduce pressure of water by encircling the outflow.

Water Conditions For Axolotl

The proper conditions for water is vital to your health, well-being and the longevity of your axolotls.

* Temperature: 60-70degF (15-23degC)

* pH: 6.5-8.0

* Chloramine and Chlorine 1 part per million

* Ammonia: 0 ppm

* Nitrite: 0 ppm

* Nitrate: 0-10 ppm

* General Hardness: 7-14 GH

* Carbonated Difficulty: 3-8 KH

Notice: The fish, shrimp amphibians and other fish that are raised in a store can adjust to different water conditions. Talk to your axolotl seller regarding the pH of the water they were raised in. Make sure your tank is prepared for this length. It is important to have an acidity that is constant.

Handling

Axolotls cannot be handled. For breathing their gills, they must remain submerged in the water. Also, they are blessed with a very delicate skin, which is covered by a mucus layer. It is possible that this layer gets removed during handling and can make the animal more susceptible to skin diseases.

Utilizing a soft-water net to quickly catch and transport an axolotl into a new container is the best technique for moving. To ensure the acclimatization process of your axolotl be sure that the temperature and other parameters of the tank you are moving to are identical to the ones in the initial tank.

If your aquarium does not have a net, then you can try to scoop or herd the fish up into the submerged tank. The tank can then be taken out of the tank. Take care when herding Axolotls because they are easily overwhelmed. If they are confronted, they'll take refuge instead of engaging with combat.

It is different from others amphibians, like those of the Pixie Frog, has not created any defense strategies. It is due to the fact that they were predators before.

Chapter 16: Axolotl Tank Preventive Maintenance

For a safe and stable atmosphere for your axolotls you'll need these items:

* Gravel vacuum

* Water testing kits

The water treatment process Scraper for algae

Every week you'll need to scrub the tank of your axolotl.

Every week, perform a 20-30% water alteration. While you're changing the water, must examine your aquarium's water conditions, scrub off any algae that isn't needed, and clean the substrate thoroughly in order to eliminate any remaining food or other debris.

Conduct

Axolotls are slow-moving, soft amphibians which tend to be active in the evenings.

Your axolotl is likely to spend most of their time on the bottom of the tank. When they are eating it is also common for them to wander around and might even follow the quarry. But, they are inactive and live an esoteric lifestyle.

If you place the sand or plant into their tank the fish may dig in and set up their surroundings. It's fascinating and interesting to watch.

Axolotls who are relaxed and relaxed will remain at ease and out of sight, whereas those who feel timid or fearful will hide. Certain axolotls might be taught in time to connect to their owners with food, and to swim up the side of the tank whenever they see their owners approaching.

In the wild, a lot of salamanders could be seen together at an event, in spite of their isolation and tendencies to wander around in solitude. When mating time is in full swing (March through June) males and females are constantly seeking each other to see if they can find each other. In addition it is rare for them to interact in a conversation.

If they're kept close, the juvenile Axolotls are known to nibble on the other and might even devour young ones.

The most effective way to reduce aggression and stress due to overpopulation is keeping animals of similar dimensions and providing sufficient space and places to hide. Every Salamander needs at least 10 liters in space.

Appearance, Colors, and Transitions

Axolotls are salamanders of the Neotenic species. They have traits that are not found in younger members of different species. It is evident by the gills of amphibians. Most amphibians shed their gills when they transition from the larva stage into adult (i.e. metamorphize). The fully mature Axolotls have three pairs of Gill stalks, which contain filaments that allow breathing behind their heads.

Apart from their gills and axolotls' horns, the primary distinct features of axolotls:

Cylindrical body. Small eyes. They are typically longer than the length of the length of the body and head together.

Axolotls in the wild can be found in a mix of green, brown and gold. They have deep purple filaments that line their gills, pupils that are black and gold Irises.

Alongside the natural species, there is many color varieties of axolotl. Due to the breeding in captivity, there is five officially recognized species of morph, placed in a chronological order below.

1. Leucism is identified by black skin, white eyes, and red Gills. Adults might develop freckles specific circumstances.

Albino Axolotls are totally white. Contrary to the leucistic shape, however the eyes and gills have pink.

3. Melanoid is much more dark than the natural species. They possess the dark black or red Irises, golden gills, or skin spots are not present.

4. Green fluorescent Protein Transgenic - looks normal under normal light, however it is glowing brilliant green when illuminated by ultraviolet light.

Golden Albino - yellow with eyes that are pink and gills with yellow eyes. Additionally, their skin is adorned with gold specks, which give them the appearance of metallic.

Axolotl Food Diet & Feeding Axolotl

In the case of feeding Axolotls, there's only four points you must be aware of

What is the diet of axolotls?

What amount of do I feed my Axolotl?

How often should I feed my an axolotl?

What is the longest time an axolotl can endure without any food?

Axolotls are carnivores that consume in wild bugs, worms, tiny fish, as well as anything else that they can squeeze into their mouths. They swallow them whole.

If you are keeping axolotls for pets, the same food must be offered. It is possible to feed them live and nonliving food. • Earthworms (live nightcrawlers) Bloodworms * brine shrimp frozen Shrimp Whiteworms; Daphnia and * Axolotl pellets and * Replica grub pie.

The amount of food you feed to your axolotl is contingent on the animal's size and age. You can gradually provide food to the animal until it is no longer eating. Axolotls can stop eating when they're full. Therefore, they can serve as a way to mark the time. Be sure to dispose of all food that is not eaten.

It is likely that you will require feeding larval and juvenile axolotls at least twice a day. Adult axolotls can be fed once a day for 2 to 3 days.

An adult who is healthy axolotl can live on its own without food for nearly two weeks.

Hand feeding Axolotls by using tongs or tweezers is suggested as it reduces the amount of waste and food that remains unassortated within the tank. Because they are nocturnal it is recommended that they be fed between two and 3 times per week and preferably during the evening. Axolotls typically consume their food as a whole so it's essential to provide them with "bite-sized" chunks.

Chapter 17: Stress

One of the main causes for sickness among axolotls can be stress. Stress can cause disease or an infection.

The most frequent sources of stress for Axolotls

* Strong current of water

* Temperatures exceeding 24 degrees Celsius.

* Non-filtered water

* Undrinkable water Tankmates

Axolotls that are stressed can be found in a variety of signs. Axolotl include a loss of appetite, and a refusal to eat regularly.

A sign that your pet is suffering from stress are the appearance of a hooked or curled toe and a forward-facing gill.

Injury

Axolotls can regenerate damaged tissue. Therefore, an absent limb need not worry you. Acute infection is the risk that you should be aware of in this case.

Wounds exposed to the sun can rapidly become infected. Therefore, you should be aware of the conditions in your water and make sure that they remain in good condition all through this period.

Impaction

Axolotls have impaction issues as their digestive system begins ineffective.

The signs of a blocked bowel are: *Refusal to consume food for several days Stool output decrease

It is crucial to ensure that you provide the axolotl with a substrate that is sand-based as this type of condition is usually resulted from the intake of stones, gravel or small pieces.

If there is an impaction situation Fridging can aid in a rapid recovery. It can also aid the animal to eliminate all harmful substances in the stomach.

Overfeeding can cause impaction as well that is why adult shouldn't be fed more frequently than once every 2 to 3 days.

Swimming Axolotls

Axolotls can swim in the air, but their excessive floating might indicate that there are air bubbles within stomach.

The only reason to concern if anxolotl cannot return to the bottom of the tank It is floating in a tizzy manner; It is often floating and appears stressed when floating.

In the same way, fridging could help eliminate the issue. In addition, it is important to examine the parameters of your water and alter these as necessary.

Infections by Microorganisms

As axolotls that are stressed and heated can get dangerous fungal and bacterial infections You should be monitoring the temperature of your water.

The most common diseases are'red leg', a bacterium which is identified by red spots on legs Columnaris in which symptoms are characterized by a lack of energy and gray patches. Saprolegnia that is distinguished by the white spots on the both the gills and skin.

Any of these issues can be tackled with salt baths or cutting.

Axolotl Fridging

Axolotls are common in areas with colder water temperatures. So, cooler temperatures could be utilized to stop the spread of illness and infections.

It also benefits impaction

To stop food from rotting, uncooked food items are ejected at lower temperatures.

In order to keep the Axolotl cool:

1. Check that your refrigerator has a temperature between 5-8 Celsius

2.Prepare the container with non-chilled chlorinated water, long enough for your axolotl's maximum length. It should be equipped with an air vent in the cover as well as enough space for your Axolotl to jump up for air.

Transfer the axolotl that is sick to the container, then protect it with a blanket to prevent light disturbance.

4. Change the old water inside the fridge with refrigerated, dechlorinated water regularly.

5. Refrigerate the axolotl until it is regenerated.

Return your axolotl's axolotl into tank water slowly before reintroducing to the tank.

Axolotl Bath in Salt

Axolotls who suffer from skin problems can be treated using salt baths and are particularly effective when combined with fridging.

Axolotls who are afflicted with fungi get a benefit from a bath in salt. Axolotls can be nursed back to health with the help of salt bath over several days.

The salt bath should be taken at least twice a day, for 10 minutes during illness.

Mix 1-2 liters of chlorinated salt with marine, aquarium and rock salt. Do not use table salt.

The water that is being utilized for icing at the similar temperature.

After it has cooled, take the fridge container and shake it vigorously.

4. The salt bath should be filled with water, then place the axolotl within.

5. Allow for a maximum of 10 minutes.

Take the tub out and then return it to the tub for thawing.

7. Repeat the process every 12 hours until your illness is completely gone and then for a further 2 to 3 days to get rid of any remaining fungal growth.

Chapter 18: What Should You Know Before Purchasing An Axolotl?

If you are planning to buy an axolotl you need to first decide if they are permitted in the state you reside in.

Axolotl ownership is not permitted within California, Maine, New Jersey as well as Virginia. A few states, including New Mexico, allow ownership however they prohibit the importation of.

It is important to research the laws for exotic animals.

If you're legally able to purchase one, then you must be advised that you'll buy a puppy which can cost anywhere from $70 around $80 dollars. Make sure that the axolotls you can purchase are fully feathered, have healthy skin that is free of injury, a consistent appetite and a pleasing style.

Breeding Axolotl

Axolotls can be quite easy to breed. However, it is important to take certain precautions in order to make sure they be successful in mating.

Axolotls can reach sexual maturity within five months to several years. It is recommended not to attempt to breed axolotls before they attain 18 months of the age of 18 months.

Female axolotls could generate more than 1000 eggs. This is quite amazing. The body prefers the production of eggs over growth and other actions.

It is important to be aware that it can be exhausting and damaging for axolotls who are young So breeding prior to 18 months of age isn't advised.

Axolotl Reproduction Methods

You can create axolotls during any season during the year, however as per some reports the most successful breeding occurs during the months of December through June.

The following research findings are:

In order to stimulate breeding In order to induce spawning University of Indiana Axolotl Colony exposed males and females to a decrease in the amount of daylight. It was a success.

It is possible to replicate these settings, however it is important to remember the fact that any part of your house that is subject to changes in the seasons (even the ones that are only partially) typically has breeding conditions.

If you live in a natural environment with plenty of sunlight, a pair of Axolotls will reproduce every year. But, be aware of the fact that they're notorious for their ability to reproduce at odd times, and at unexpected

intervals.

Establishing an Axolotl Breeding Aquarium

Your aquarium should be stocked with a variety of silk and living plants to ensure that females can have a spot for their eggs.

Also, small chunks of slate or stone are recommended to be placed at the base of your tank for males to have an area to place spermatophores.

Axolotl Mating and Reproduction

Males begin reproduction. They deposit between 5 to 25 spermatophores on rocks as well as other items within their surroundings.

In a typical mating process Axolotl males raise their tails, and then make violent movements of writhing towards females when he drags her across the tank towards the spermatophores which he's set up.

They will be collected to fertilize her internal system. take place.

In the hours that are between two and three days later, she'll lay her eggs in a single layer in the form of rocks, plant leaves as well as scattered around the aquarium.

The female can lay as many as 1,000 eggs per the time she spawns.

Incubating Axolotl Eggs

In a couple of hours the albino morph eggs will appear bright white. Regular eggs will have dark brown.

Within two or three weeks, the eggs will hatch and transform into the larvae of an axolotl.

Make sure that eggs are well-aerated. An air compressor could aid in this. If the temperature is 20 ° Celsius eggs are expected to develop in between 14 and 17 days.

Are Axolotls Appropriate For You?

If you're able to set up the correct tank, water condition and food for an axolotl one is sure to bring you a quantity of fun.

Chapter 19: What Are Axolotls?

Axolotls are amphibians belonging to the Caudata family of animals, which includes salamanders and Newts. There are about 8000 species of amphibians all, and the majority occur in tropical regions. Amphibians' skins are porous most of their larvae have a stage also known as a Tadpole and is born from eggs that have been placed within waters.

It is believed that the Axolotl is a species of salamander that has a unique genetic structure. It's a paedomorphic salamander which is akin to an Tiger salamander. They maintain the majority of their traits as larvae throughout adulthood because of a rare disease called 'neoteny' which is why they display all traits that a tadpole would have including feathery gills and the long dorsal fin with a quill-like shape even after they have fully developed.

Axolotls often mistakenly thought to be fishermen, can be described as the sole amphibians who live their entire existence in the water. Based on their look and their preferred habitat, axolotls are also known as Mexican walking fish.

The Aztecs discovered a massive salamander living on the shores of the island that they built their capital city of Tenochtitlan as they first arrived at the Valley of Mexico in the 13th century. In honor of Xolotl who was their god of lightning and fire they gave the salamander the name "axolotl." To prevent being sacrificed, Xolotl was claimed to transform into a salamander in addition to various other types. The man was captured and executed eventually.

Axolotls For instance, were frequently killed as food in the time of the Aztecs and still eaten by the Aztecs in Mexico even today. They've also grown to be among the most loved pets around the globe due to their low maintenance requirements and their charming. Scientists are intrigued by the creatures due to their extraordinary capacity to regenerate. In contrast salamanders are nearly gone extinct in their natural habitat.

Axolotls shouldn't be confused with the stage of larvae of the tiger salamander, which is closely related to it species (A. Tigrinum) They are found throughout North America and can turn paedomorphic in a few instances. Also, they should not be mistaken for Mudpuppies (Necturus spp.) or aquatic salamanders belonging to an entirely separate group that do not have a close relationship with the axolotls however they appear like them.

The Axolotl resided in a variety of lakes in the Mexico Valley, but many areas have been drained and have become polluted. Lake Xochimilco and its wetlands is the sole place that axolotls are found. Development of the human race, dumping of waste as well as habitat destruction as well as climate change are the most significant causes of Amphibian decline.

The Axolotls (Ambystoma mexicanum) belong to the Ambystomatidae family that includes only one extinct species. The Ambystoma family, often referred to as mole salamanders more than 30 species salamanders. Axolotls could reach a length of nine inches (20 centimeters) as a rule, but certain species have surpassed twelve inches (30 centimeters). Salamanders kept in captivity can live between 5 and 6 years, but certain species have lived for up to 17 years.

Between the ages of 18 and 27 months, an sexually mature axolotl could grow to between 15 and 45 centimeters (6-18 inches) in length and a length of approximately 23 centimeters (9 in) being the most typical with more than 30cm (12 in) as it is atypical. External gills, as well as an extended caudal fin between the head and the vent differentiate axolotls from salamander larvae. As salamanders mature generally, they shed their gills on the outside, whereas the Axolotl retains these. It is because of axolotls Neoteny evolution that has led to them being much more aquatic than the other species of salamanders.

The eyes of these animals are not lidless while their skulls appear huge. Their legs aren't developed and their digits are long and slim. Males are identified by the inflated cloacae, which are covered with papillae. females can be distinguished by their larger bodies that are stuffed with eggs. The external Gill stalks (rami) extend from the back of their head and function to carry oxygenated water. External gill rami are covered by filaments (fimbriae). Four-gill slits laced with gill rakers keep food particles from getting under the external gills, while also allowing particles to flow through.

Axolotls are great pet breeds.

1. Axolotls are cute.

Axolotls are popular pets due to of their friendly nature. In the case of this adorable salamander, there is a wide range of colours that you can choose from. It is possible to have an Axolotl which blooms with the color that you like. Albino varieties are also renowned for their distinct design of white and red. The cost is usually higher to buy an albino version that is not. The mottled brown, infrarot, the melanoid as well as the leucistic white with black and red gills eyes are other popular choices.

Check out GFP Axolotls, if you're looking for something distinctive. They sparkle under the black sunlight, due to their genetically altered.

2. You don't require a large tank.

A single Axolotl is sure to be happy in a wide 20-gallon tank. Since they live in the soil, they is bound to be massive. They don't care about the upper layer of the tank. They are content to walk over the sandy surface. If you're planning to house two Axolotls then you'll require an aquarium that is 40 gallon. If you only have one salamander, most owners advocate a 10 gallon tank. If you really would like your pet to be successful then you must raise the amount by two.

An increased capacity tank means that you don't need to change the water every so often.

3. There's No Need for a Heater

Axolotls should be kept in an aquarium at home with cold waters. The best temperature to keep them is between 60 and 70 degrees Fahrenheit. Based on this, it is possible to buy an air cooler in case your aquarium's water isn't cold enough. If you're not planning to purchase one, but your home isn't equipped with cold spots, we suggest maintaining the Axolotl at the bottom of your basement.

4. Axolotls are simple to care for.

The Axolotl is a animal that will eat anything that he can get the chance to eat. The food doesn't need to be edible. This is why you should not make use of a substrate with coarse grains. It is beneficial if you provided them with meat-based food because they're carnivores. Protein is necessary for their growth. Sinking pellets that are specifically designed for carnivores are perfect for their needs. Bloodworms, Shrimp and earthworms are good sources of protein. Pellets that are specifically made to be used by Axolotls are available in all pet stores.

It is possible to feed it using your hands, even if the bite does hurt it'll feel similar to Sandpaper on your skin, and is not likely to cause injury.

5. Axolotls are peaceful animals.

Although Axolotls can be predators, they can appear hostile when trying to capture their prey. They do it because they are in need of it They are quite tranquil (especially when they are domesticated). If they're not doing anything generally, they wander around the bottom of the aquarium, looking for clues. They're calm and tranquil species.

If you have two fish within the same tank, it will cause any territorial issues. In the event, however you've purchased enough fish tanks of sufficient size.

This is just one reasons it is a good idea to purchase an Axolotl to your aquarium. In the end, who doesn't prefer a pet that's unique and simple to take care of? It will be a pleasure to display this animal to all your acquaintances, whose distinctive characteristics will be enthralling.

It's easy to feed them, create an aquarium for them and you can even breed them. If you'd like breeding them then you could choose from a variety of colors. Although Axolotls tend to be solitary animals they can be kept with two in one tank, or a number of them within different tanks. Concerning security, they're completely poison-free.

Where do Axolotls where do they live?

The wild axolotls are only discovered in the marshy ruins in Lake Xochimilco and the canals which lead to it, on Mexico City's southern border. Lake Chalco, another of Mexico City's five "big lakes" where the early Aztecs lived, was once home to axolotls, too. Based on NBC News, except for Xochimilco the other five lakes were cleaned out during the 1970s in order to limit flooding and permit expansion of urban areas.

Axolotls' carnivorous diet is a fact that has placed them historically on the top in the food chain. Mollusks, fish and arthropods like spiders and insects are among the animals they hunt for. And, even more importantly, they eat one another. According to an JSTOR Daily report that it was reported that the United Nations Food and Agricultural Organization introduced carp and tilapia fish into the area of salamanders in the late 1970s and early 1980s to give residents greater food. The fish feed on the young axolotls as well as pose a serious danger for salamanders.

Similar to all Ambystoma species that live in Mexico, Axolotls are members of the tiger salamander also known as Ambystoma Tigrinum the species complex. Similar to other species of neotenic that live in higher altitude water body that is surrounded by an extremely hazardous terrain. This is thought to promote Neoteny. But, in the Axolotl ecosystem, a terrestrial colony of Mexican Tiger salamanders exists and reproduces.

The result of development of Mexico City and the resulting contamination of waterways, as well as introduced exotic species like perch and tilapia, wild Axolotls are on the brink of being extinct before 2020. They are listed as critically endangered by the International Union for Conservation of Nature and Natural Resources (IUCN) classified the species as critically endangered in the wild, and has an estimated decline of 100 to 1000 adult individuals. They are included in Appendix II of Convention on International Trade in Endangered Species (CITES). Axolotls are commonly used for research because of their ability to grow the limbs, gills and portions of their eyes and brains.

Chapter 20: What Are The Various Types Of Axolotls?

Based on estimates, currently there are about 20 different variations of Axolotl colors that can be kept as pets. Axolotls are without doubt among the most adorable pets that you can own. Axolotls might be a good choice for the most beautiful exotic pet of all time due to their cute appearance as well as the creative the gills.

Since the past few years, these tiny frogs from the water have been increasingly popular with pet owners around the world. They have received more notice due to the fact that Yolanda Buenaventura appeared in the popular comedy Bo Jack Horseman.

The primary reason to be interested, however it is due to the baffling hue changes we'll discuss in detail on this day. Numerous color variations were created due to breeding. Some of them are scarcer and better value.

Axolotls are colored by two distinct genes, each one derived from a parent. The gene itself is broken down into three parts that are each for three kinds of the chromatophores (see the table below). Alleles refer to these components. The quantity of different chromatophore kinds that occur in the epidermis of an axolotl's is affected by the mix of alleles. It can increase or diminishes the hue. The albino alleles include, for instance, codes for a small amount of melanophores on the skin. Melanophores usually produce a dark brown skin tone. However, they appear to be a prominent white color in this particular person.

A black axolotl is a different instance. Alleles in melanoid-axolotls cause more melanophores and result in a species that is black. Certain colour patterns are only able to be recognized if the individual axolotl is born with two alleles of each parent.

Axolotls who have an albino allele as well as a normal allele, aren't albino. For albino color to be displayed, it is necessary to have two versions of albino genes. It can result in breeding for certain shades more challenging as compared to breeding for other hues as well as influence how scarce specific varieties are. Most morphs are based on an alteration in the colour of the allele that results in a distinct color or design. The same thing can happen with snakes, with Ball Python Morphs being an great illustration. It is a great deal of time and effort as well as carefully bred breeding to produce the colour-changing morph of an individual mutant. The breeding and care of the pet becomes more well-known, new breeds are constantly being discovered.

Most popular are:

Leucistic

Axolotls sporting sparkling gold flecks with pink or red eyes, eye color that is dark brown or black are considered leucistic. They're quite scarce in nature due to the danger they pose to predators but they're one of the most frequently seen and beautiful varieties in the captive environment. It is like albino axolotls from their appearance. But, albino axolotls do feature red eyes.

Leucism can be caused by one mutation which results in the production of less melanocytes. The Axolotls who have this mutation don't show similar patterns to the wild type morph, because melanocytes make melanin, which is a dark pigment.

Golden Albino

Golden albinos are available in a variety of colors, which range from pure white to pale yellow and orange-gold. Their bodies are covered with sparkling dots and their eyes are either white either yellow or white. Additionally, they have yellower eyes that have a peachy the colour.

They're indistinguishable from albinos who are white as children They share the sensitivities to bright lights. When they get older, will they begin to develop a beautiful golden hue. The golden albino morph is, as with many of the other light-coloured Axolotls in this list is devoid of melanophores. The morph stands out since it has xanthophores which give it a golden yellow hue. Iridophores with multiple iridophores could seem to be covered in gold leaf.

Wild-type

Axolotls in the wild are an eerie dark green with olive and black mottling. They also sport a light belly, and gold speckles that are derived due to the Iridophores. They're similar colors and patterns that are found in wild-caught species. This is the most commonly used and longest-running color for pet owners.

In 1863, the very first wild type axolotls were introduced to Europe. Based on the particular species, wild axolotls may be gray, black or even a lighter yellow-green color. The gill filaments are purple and the gold irises with black eyes are distinctive since their hue may blend with the murky lakebeds that surround Mexico City.

Piebald

Piebalds sport dark grey, black, or black symmetrical spots on their backs and faces with red gills and black eyes and deep grey, dark green or black grils. They can also extend down their sides as well as legs, but are not common. The patterns are mostly limited to the upper part of the body.

The gene for piebald is hereditary however it is extremely rare, with the majority of breeders located within New Zealand. When the axolotl becomes older, this pattern becomes darker, leading to an axolotl with a white and black salamander.

This is a morphological leucistic with melanophores concentrating on their backs and head. Cells that migrate in particular directions called neural crest cells in embryogenesis results in this.

Mosaic

Mosaic axolotls sport the appearance of white, black and gold specks of color on their bodies. They could also sport the gills of a purple and red stripe and bright eyes. Most mosaics contain a mixture of albino and melanistic parents.

They're composed of two eggs which are fusioned into one. Instead of being separated into halves, each cell has the colors of the parents in random order. It creates a striking individual axolotl colour.

Mosaics are not breed. They are rare and seldom available, however they might appear on occasion.

Copper

Axolotls that have copper-colored freckles as well as grey irises are characterized by a gray body. The gills of their genitals are grayish-red and their belly is thinner. Copper axolotls are available in many shades, ranging that range from caramel to almost pink. This is a popular morph at the places where they're being sold because of their beautiful face, speckled appearance and sandy coloring. The first copper axolotls were bred within the United States and Australia. Others have a much harder time locating the breed.

The copper morph is one of the forms of albinism which is more mild. It has lower levels of melanin and pteridines. However, they're not completely devoid of these pigments. Coppers can be crossed with other morphs in order to create distinct variations in the melanoid copper as well as axanthic copper.

Lavender

The lavender axolotl is the appearance of a silvery, faint color with greyish-red eyes and eyes of black. They also coat their bodies with grey spots, hence their Dalmatian title of silver!

Certain varieties of lavender mature to the green or grey hue however, the majority remain in the purple. The melanoid varieties of lavender, which possess a darker shade of purple without spots, can also be produced.

The combination of these colours, but it is not very common.

The morphs of lavender are mostly seen only in the United States and have only seen a few instances. Their soft, purple tint and their polka-dotted design are highly sought-after despite the fact that they are scarce.

Black Melanoid

The recessive mutation was first discovered in a lab for the first time in the year 1961 and has become widespread. Albinos form the opposite to black Melanoids. Melanoid species are less melanophores, and higher levels of iridophores.

There are a range of colors that range from dark green to completely black with gills that are dark purple. A majority of melanoids possess a purple or grey belly. Certain individuals look like the black wild-type axolotls, but do not have the shining golden iris common for wild Axolotls.

The substrate that you use black melanoids may change color tones. The change in colour isn't lasting The colour of your axolotl is likely to change depending on the material. The colour of your axolotl will become brighter with an un-light substrate, such as white sand.

Chapter 21: White Albino

White albinos possess white or red gill filaments. They also have eyelids that are white or pink and golden specks of light on their stalks of the gills, and are completely white. Albinos that are young and white, specifically around their belly, may seem almost transparent. Iridophores that line their gills develop a darker red color as they age, while the remainder of their body is completely white. There aren't any xanthophores nor melanophores found in this species.

Even though they possess iridophores the cells can only be found within the Gills. Albinos with white albinos look like leucistic axolotl on the outside, however they do not have color within their eyes. Because of this, white albinos are more sensitive light and also have less vision over other axolotl species.

Speckled Leucistic

Axolotls that have speckled mutations are a type of leucistic mutation. They have dark green, black, or brown speckles that appear on their heads, tails as well as their backs. Their main colour is white. This is similar to the typical leucistic morphs. However, the amount of speckles isn't as intense as the mosaic or piebald forms.

The axolotl typically appears like a leucistic in the beginning, but is spotted later in life. The cells that produce pigment develop when they age, which allows them to alter their color and patterns of freckles.

Chimera

Due to the fact that Chimeras are Chimera is extremely rare It is a question of whether or not it is worthy of recognition as a morph that is real. Chimeras possess two different morphs, one in one part of their bodies. One is to the second. It's divided in two parts, one left, and one to the right. Half albino and half wild type Chimaeras have appeared so in the past. Chimera axolotls form when two egg embryos combine into one. Because the eggs didn't fuse completely the majority of them do not hatch.

Chimeras are not bred selectively because they're a developmental issue that's not attributable to genetics.

Heavily-Marked Melanoid

The melanoid with the most prominent markings is an distinct variant of the melanoid with black markings.

Normal black melanoids have dark and black dots that contain small yellow and light green patches. This variant has been seen a handful of instances, but nothing is currently known about the condition. Since it is impossible to predict the possibility that two parents with melanoid genes will produce offspring with a strong mark These colour variations are very rare.

Green Fluorescent Protein

On first sight the Green Fluorescent Protein Axolotls seem to be a different form. But, if subjected to UV radiation, they change to an enthralling glowing green. In normal daylight the effect is not noticeable however, in UV light, it's evident. Skinny people like albino or leucistic persons, display an even, flawless look.

The gene for green fluorescent protein was found in jellyfish, and was then intentionally incorporated to the genome of the axolotl. Researchers from Max Planck Institute Max Planck Institute generated this mutation in 2005 to study cell mobility as well as cancer.

Firefly

Lloyd Strohl invented the Firefly axolotls to create an intentionally-designed model. Embryonic graphing was initially utilized to investigate regeneration of the limbs. There are some disagreements about whether it is appropriate to be employed to breed pets.

Chapter 22: What Are The Uncommon And Rare Axolotl Morphs?

Due to the rarity of it due to its rarity Axolotls are an extremely popular choice with Axolotl owners. The morph is scarce however it is easy to obtain since GFP Axolotls are popular breeders. All Axolotl that is genetically altered to bear GFP Green Fluorescent Protein Gene is called an GFP Axolotl. As a result of the process of protein synthesis GFP Axolotls will be green when exposed to ultraviolet lighting. GFP appears to be a second form of.

There's nothing such that is an GFP Axolotl. Another morph is the Axolotl. There is a possibility of having an GFP Leucistic Axolotl as an instance. It is possible that the GFP gene can be handed down through generations. Lighter-colored Axolotls that carry the gene are more brightly.

Because of the red color in their eyes, copper Morphs can be mistaken for Albino Axolotls. The majority of them are pale brown, and they have black markings. This type of morph can be difficult to spot as compared to other types.

Chimera Axolotls can be described as Axolotls created by the union between two eggs. The result is the creation of an Axolotl having a different form on one side of the body and a different one in the other. There's a split in colour. Due to the fact that one aspect of the Axolotl Axolotl may develop more quickly than the other side, it's highly unlikely that the morph will endure. It's difficult to deliberately cultivate this type of type of mutation.

Mosaic Morphs appear to be similar to chimaera Axolotls in the sense that they're an amalgamation of two morphs. However, they're not exactly divided in two halves. They are generally sterile as they're made of two cells, which arise during the development process. It is also impossible to deliberately reproduce the form.

Piebald Morphs have more dark pigmentation along the side of their bodies as well as the head's tops. In comparison to normal Axolotls that have spots, the spots of Piebald Morphs are deeper and more full. The morph's color is transferred down the generations.

The Lavender Morph can be another alternative. It can be difficult to find. Axolotls which have a color of purple with black markings are referred to as morphs that have a lavender hue.

The breeder who owns the breed is the sole one to acquire Firefly Morphs, who can make use of the breed to study before selling them for sale. By using embryonic graphing Lloyd Stroh II constructed this special Morph. Normal breeding cannot produce this specific morph. Axolotls that have an elongated tail will have a dark tail. Those that have a dark tail will be the light tail.

www.ingramcontent.com/pod-product-compliance
Lightning Source LLC
Chambersburg PA
CBHW071332120626
46546CB00002B/532